CHALLENGERS AND CHARGERS

CHALLENGERS AND CHARGERS

A HISTORY OF
THE LIFE GUARDS
1945 - 1992

by
WILLIAM LOYD

with a foreword by
Major General Lord Michael Fitzalan Howard
GCVO, CB, CBE, MC.

LEO COOPER

LONDON

First published in Great Britain in 1992 by
LEO COOPER
190 Shaftesbury Avenue, London WC2H 8JL
an imprint of
Pen & Sword Books Ltd,
47 Church Street, Barnsley, South Yorkshire S70 2AS

A CIP catalogue record for this book is available
from the British Library.

ISBN: 8 85052 353 2

Typeset by Yorkshire Web, Barnsley, S. Yorks.
in Garamond 10 point

Printed by
Redwood Press
Melksham, Wiltshire

CONTENTS

To the memory of Shylock:
the finest black horse of them all

Acknowledgements

I would like to thank all of the many past members and the handful of serving members of The Life Guards for providing me with the many anecdotes and photographs which go to make up this book. They are too numerous to mention here, but all can be found in the text.

I must express my gratitude for the faith placed in me by the past and present serving officers who agreed to sponsor this book, namely Captain the Duke of Marlborough, Sir Philip Naylor-Leyland, Bart, Captain Hon Robin Cayzer, Dr Hon Gilbert Greenall, Major Timothy Gooch, Lieutenant Colonels James Ellery and Dennis Meakin and Major Peter Hunter.

Past and serving officers read my draft chapters and their resulting comments put me right on many occasions. For this my particular thanks must go to Major General Sir Simon Cooper, Brigadier Arthur Gooch, Colonel WH Gerard Leigh, Lieutenant Colonels James Ellery and Dennis Meakin, Majors Toni Chiesman and Timothy Gooch and Captains Michael Naylor-Leyland, David Palmer and Derek Stratford.

Major Paddy Kersting, curator of the Household Cavalry Museum, and his assistant Mr Ted Woodbridge, both former Blues, allowed me access to their archives, and I had great help from all at Headquarters, Household Cavalry. *The Guards Magazine* (formerly the *Household Brigade Magazine*), of which Lieutenant Colonel Sir Julian Paget, Bart, has been editor for many years, has been a most useful source for reference, as has been the regiment's annual *Acorn Magazine*.

I would like to thank Tom Hartman for his painstaking editing of my manuscript; also Jonathan Grosvenor of Ivanhoe Publishing for the use of his Apple Macintosh computer without which the preparation of this book would not have been possible. Finally my heart-felt thanks to my wife Lilo for her hours of patient proof-reading.

Foreword

by Major General Lord Michael Fitzalan Howard GCVO, CB, CBE, MC, Colonel, The Life Guards, from 1979 onwards.

No account of the activities and achievements of The Life Guards has been written since the two volumes which recorded the history of the First and Second Household Cavalry Regiments in the Second World War. Much has happened to the Regiment since they reformed as The Life Guards in August, 1945, and it is important that a volume should be produced as a chronicle of the many and varied places where Life Guards have served, from Goslar to Kuwait.

Major William Loyd was given the monumental task of writing the story of the Regiment as they moved in and out of Cold War tasks and training in Germany and other parts of Western Europe and Canada. Included are world-wide operational duties in Egypt, the Arab Emirates, Oman and Aden, in Borneo, Malaya, Hong Kong, Cyprus and Belize, in Northern Ireland, and most recently back in the desert for the Gulf War.

Despite forty-six years of peace, the Regiment has been fully engaged in minor wars and counter-terrorism; in peace-keeping with the United Nations; in aid to the Civil Power in the firemen's and ambulancemen's disputes; in anti-terrorist duties such as those at Heathrow and Gatwick airports; and, of course until recently, in countering the threat posed by the forces of the Warsaw Pact.

The Life Guards have been organized as an armoured car regiment, an airportable regiment, an armoured reconnaissance regiment, an armoured regiment and have met, year in year out, their commitment to Public Duties with the Household Cavalry Mounted Regiment.

It is using these bare facts that William Loyd has so skilfully described the history of The Life Guards and those who have served in the Regiment since 1945. It is, above all, a story about people: the fun and excitement, the good times and the bad through which officers and soldiers have carried out their duties with renowned skill, determination and humour.

The Regiment have a reputation second to none in their service to the Crown and to the Nation. The last forty-six years have continued to enhance their standing won in over 300 years as the senior regiment of the British Army.

Today, as The Life Guards stand at the beginning of a new venture in partnership with The Blues and Royals, it is worth repeating the words of Colonel Humphrey Wyndham at the close of his history of the First Household Cavalry Regiment: 'The spirit and tradition of the two regiments has become merged into those of two armoured car regiments. Both officers and men still retained the same characteristics that had distinguished their predecessors of The Life Guards and Blues, but for six years their whole scheme of things had centred around 1 and 2 HCR.'

In the years to come our scheme of things, with those of The Blues and Royals, will centre around the armoured reconnaissance and mounted regiments. But The Life Guards will retain their spirit and the traditions that have characterized the Regiment since 1660; this is epitomized by the preservation of uniforms and customs within The Life Guards' sabre and mounted squadrons of the new Household Cavalry organization.

I commend this new history as an excellent addition to the uniquely distinguished record of The Life Guards.

Preface

This is a book about several thousand British men who, at some time between the end of the Second World War in Europe in May, 1945, and the union of the Regiment with The Blues and Royals in October, 1992 to form the Household Cavalry Regiment, wore the cap-badge of The Life Guards. Some conscripts may have done so reluctantly, but I think that most of the gentlemen of The Life Guards, as they were so addressed, wore the badge with pride.

The Life Guards, formed in 1660 and the senior regiment in the British Army, did not question why they were sent to various strange places and called upon at times to separate one set of indigenous inhabitants who were 'good' from another set who were 'bad'. It was their practice to do what was required, and do it well, then have a bit of a whinge about it afterwards. This applies to all ranks: a former Commanding Officer even admitted to me that he was not clear as to why his command had been in a certain place at a certain time.

Some Life Guards, such as Major Generals Sir Desmond Langley and Sir Simon Cooper, made the army their career: others went on to other walks of life, their service done. Some made their names in politics, in industry, or in the sporting world: a few others, inevitably, deviated from the legal or moral codes, but all would agree that once a Life Guard, always a Life Guard.

During the forty-seven years under review The Life Guards, in common with the rest of the British Armed Forces, spent a great deal of time in training for war against possible aggression by the now defunct Warsaw Pact block of the Soviet Union and the countries of Eastern Europe. The fact that the Warsaw Pact was the first to lose its resolve and to disband must be due, at any rate in part, to the will to maintain a high standard of training for war within the NATO Armed Forces. This high standard was to show its worth both in the British Falklands campaign of 1982, in which elements of The Blues and Royals took part, and in the 1991 War in the Gulf in which the entire regiment of Life Guards were deployed as part of the coalition forces arrayed against Iraq.

A group of people who receive no mention in these pages, space being at a premium, are the wives. Theirs was not always a happy lot, for, apart from Germany and the Far East, the foreign tours of duty were almost invariably unaccompanied postings. For a wife to bid farewell to her man from Windsor as he departs on a comparatively low-risk posting such as Cyprus today is one thing. To see him off for an emergency tour in Ulster from a garrison town in Germany, far from familiar surroundings, must be quite another.

By and large the women who followed the drum were a stoic lot; when their men were away they drew strength from one another and concentrated on raising their children; when their men returned, they welcomed them home. If the hand that rocked the cradle did not exactly rule The Life Guards, then the stability that the wives provided went a long way to adding to the overall efficiency of the Regiment.

The Life Guards with whom I served seemed reasonably confident that British was best, and totally confident that The Life Guards were undoubtedly the best regiment of them all. I believe that they were right.

Oxford
June 1992

Glossary

The majority of terms used in this book are, or were, in common usage in the Army during the period under review. Below are listed those which are peculiar to the Household Cavalry, in particular to The Life Guards, with definitions, or comparisons to their equivalents in infantry battalions :

Blues, Blues and Royals	The Royal Horse Guards (The Blues) were the junior of the two regiments of Household Cavalry. They were amalgamated with the Royal Dragoons (the Royals) in February 1969 to form The Blues and Royals.
Chuff chart	A self-made reverse calendar showing the days remaining of a conscript's service, which would then be ticked off day by day.
Cornet	2nd Lieutenant in The Blues, or in The Blues and Royals.
Corporal of Horse	Sergeant
Corporal Major	Sergeant Major, but also used as an honorific title to Staff Corporals holding SQMC appointments.
CVR	Combat vehicle, reconnaissance, either (T), tracked, or (W), wheeled.
Depot	Combermere Barracks, Windsor, until 1966, thereafter the Guards Depot at Pirbright.
Director of Music	Bandmaster, however of Commissioned rank.
Dutyman	A trooper posted to ceremonial duty in London
Egyptian PT	Sleep.
Gold Stick	Gold Stick in Waiting, a Court appointment held on alternate months by the Colonels of the two regiments of Household Cavalry.
Inns of Court	Inns of Court and City Yeomanry (TA)
Knightsbridge	Hyde Park Barracks, London SW7. Location of the Household Cavalry Mounted Regiment.
(LE)	Used after an individual's rank to denote Late Entry to the commissioned rank, in much the same way as (QM) used to be used for those holding a Quartermaster commission.

Line Cavalry	The cavalry regiments of the Royal Armoured Corps.
Medical Officer	Unusually in the Household Cavalry these doctors would be part of the regimental strength, and cap-badged accordingly.
Mounted Duty	Service with the Mounted Regiment.
Mounted Regiment	The composite regiment of both Life Guards and Blues and Royals on ceremonial duty and stationed in London.
Musician	Bandsman, an appointment.
Officers' House	Officers' Mess, if in a building.
Pirbright	The Guards Depot.
Queen's Life Guard	The ceremonial mounted guard provided alternately by The Life Guards and The Blues and Royals over Horse Guards Arch in Whitehall.
Sabre Squadron	Rifle Company.
Sabre Troop	Rifle Platoon.
Sheriff	Corporal of Horse in charge of the regimental provost staff.
Silver Stick	Silver Stick in Waiting, a Court appointment held *ex officio* by the Lieutenant Colonel Commanding the Household Cavalry.
Silver Stick Adjutant	A further Court appointment, held by the Regimental Adjutant at Headquarters, Household Cavalry.
Squadron Corporal Major	Company Sergeant Major.
Squadron Quartermaster Corporal (SQMC)	Company Quartermaster Sergeant
Staff Corporal	Staff Sergeant.
Swan	To drive around without any obvious purpose
Windsor	Combermere Barracks and associated buildings in Windsor.
Woodentop Farm	Life Guard slang for the Guards Depot.
Woodentops	The Footguards who live therein.

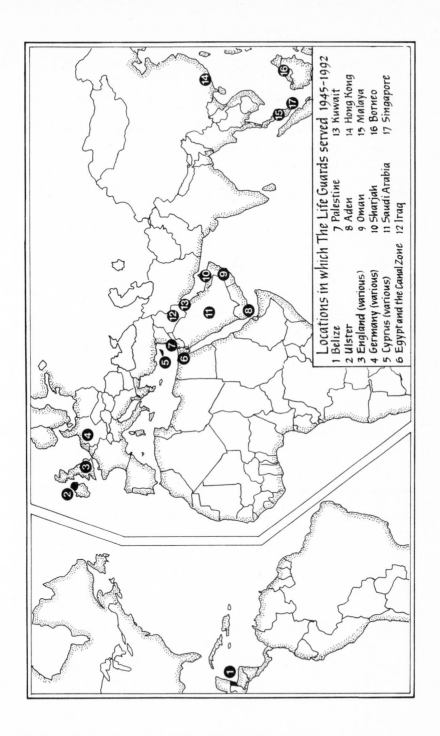

Locations in which The Life Guards served 1945-1992

1 Belize
2 Ulster
3 England (various)
4 Germany (various)
5 Cyprus (various)
6 Egypt and the Canal Zone
7 Palestine
8 Aden
9 Oman
10 Sharjah
11 Saudi Arabia
12 Iraq
13 Kuwait
14 Hong Kong
15 Malaya
16 Borneo
17 Singapore

Author's Notes

1. The Household Cavalry, in common with the rest of the army, makes great use of nicknames. Indeed, at the time of writing, three colonels in The Blues and Royals are trying in vain to lose the agnomina Fluffie, Dozie and Bingles, all acquired in early service. Nicknames are usually only used between those of roughly equal rank, so, with exceptions such as 'Boy','G' and 'Bunker', which were practically universal, if not always to the individuals' faces, they have not always been used.

2. Subalterns are never referred to by their ranks, eg Lieutenant or 2nd Lieutenant; however, I have shown them us such in the text for the sake of clarity.

3. I have tried where possible to give Christian names as well as ranks to individuals. I hasten to reassure the older readers that Regimental Corporal Majors are still firmly 'Sir' to all of their subordinates and 'Mr.' to all officers, in the same way that Commanding Officers are invariably addressed as 'Colonel' or 'Colonel, Sir'.

Part I

THE AGE OF THE CONSCRIPT

Chapter 1

From Berlin to Cairo (1945-1947)

'WHAT actually happened was that, one sunny morning in July (1945), I set off from Goslar, in Germany, with some 350 Blues for Colonel Henry Abel Smith on the Rhine,' said Lieutenant Colonel F.E.B. 'Boy' Wignall, in his address to The Life Guards' Association dinner during the following year. 'And I returned three days later with 350 Life Guards.'

So The Life Guards were re-integrated as a regiment after six years of war during which they had, with The Blues, formed the 1st and 2nd Household Cavalry Regiments. Was this a happy occasion? Apparently it was not. The majority of the fifty-two officers and 900 men had joined since the outbreak of war, moreover many had formed close friendships with their comrades in The Blues. However, when Colonel Hon. Humphrey Wyndham MC, who had commanded the Regiment before the war and was now in the uniform of a press correspondent, dropped in on them a month later in Goslar, he was full of praise for the 'spirit undaunted and unimpaired'.

Those Life Guards who had been with the 1st Household Cavalry Regiment had gone to war in January, 1940, with their horses, and had not been mechanized until the following year. After seeing action in the Middle East, North Africa and in Italy over the next five years, they found themselves by coincidence flanking the 2nd Regiment as the armoured car screen to Lieutenant General Sir Brian Horrocks' XXX Corps as the Allies drove towards Berlin. The political decision, which was to be the cause of so much trouble over the next forty-five years, to allow the Soviet Red Army to take the city, and the German unconditional surrender on Saturday 5 May, 1945, saw both regiments short of their objective. (The Regiments had the frustration, together with the rest of the division, of being halted for ten days in their advance on the city to allow this to happen.)

The 1st Regiment ended the war with the Guards Armoured Division at Stade on the Elbe estuary, while the 2nd Regiment entered the German naval base at Cuxhaven on VE (Victory in Europe) Day. Trooper Glyn Randall, a Life Guard with the 1st Regiment, well remembers the memorial service which was held soon afterwards for the nine men killed in what was, for the 1st Regiment, a six-week campaign in Europe. The last man to die was probably Corporal of Horse Troughton, a family man who had gone through the whole war, only to be struck by a stray bullet on the day before the armistice.

Glyn Randall also remembers receiving 'a terrible ticking off for carrying too many of the lads on my (Dingo) scout car to view the heaps of bodies in undignified death, wearing their blue-striped camp uniforms' at a concentration camp in the Soltau area, which would have been Belsen. His elder brother John was also a trooper with the Regiment, and remembers handing despatches out of the back of the wireless truck to one Corporal Lloyd, later Regimental Corporal Major, who was a despatch rider at the time.

Corporal Eric Lloyd was promoted to Corporal of Horse in charge of the regimental provost staff while the Regiment was at Goslar. One of his duties as 'Sheriff' was to remove German civilians, usually female, from disused bunkers on the camp perimeter. So 'Bunker' became his nickname, and has been so ever since.

It must have been around this time that the Officers' House acquired its best-known belonging of the present century: the Dry Roger. This charming wood-carving of a man and a woman embracing, believed to be after Rodin's 'The Kiss', possibly by Arno Breker, was looted from a house in Goslar in which RHQ and B Squadron were quartered. An attempt was made, in the 'seventies, to identify the culprit; however, Majors Kenneth Diacre and Derek Cooper and Captain Jack Creswell all happily blamed each other, while Major Robin Wordsworth held a minority opinion that A Squadron were responsible, and that the theft had been from Wolfenbüttel.

Provenance apart, the little carving has travelled the world with the Regiment, from Singapore to Belfast. The lady suffered chipped toes in Major Michael Young's car on the way back from Cyprus; the couple both emerged the worse for wear after being left to soak in the bath in Palestine by Lieutenant Colonel Tony Meredith-Hardy; and Brigadier Muir Turnbull remembers trying to improve on the craftsman's art by the temporary addition of some crudely carved pieces of cork.

The Regiment stayed in Wolfenbüttel for the remainder of the year. Initially non-fraternization was enforced, indeed some soldiers received detention for fraternization. However this was revoked in September, with the only provisos that no soldier could marry, or be billetted with, German nationals. Also enforced was a ban on any wives coming out to Germany. This was, not surprisingly, very unpopular with the married men, but the situation in Germany during that first winter, with no form of civilian government, 2½ million prisoners-of-war and about 1 million 'displaced persons', coupled with severe weather, was critical.

The Life Guards were responsible for patrolling the divisional area and dealing with incidents as they occurred. B Squadron in particular were detached and sent down to Springe, south of Hanover, when civil unrest was threatened. The hard winter, though ideal for skiing by all ranks in the Hartz mountains, was then followed by bad flooding in the spring, Wolfenbüttel itself being under threat of inundation for a twenty-four hour period.

The Regiment finally reached Berlin in March, 1946, and were located in great comfort in Kladow Barracks, a former Luftwaffe base on the edge of the Wannsee. The Commanding Officer even made the point at the Association dinner that perhaps the soldiers would expect something rather similar when they came home. He could hardly have had Combermere Barracks, Windsor, in mind: they were virtually unchanged after being rebuilt in the 1860s. (The previous occupants of the Berlin barracks, one of the [British] Royal Tank regiments, had built up the civilian staff to a level that, numerically, matched their own!)

It was around this time that Major Tom Hanbury left on Class A release. While serving with the 2nd Household Cavalry Regiment he had been awarded an MC; Corporal of Horse 'Tommy' Thompson, later to become Riding Master, won a DCM and Corporal Brooks the Military Medal for a spirited action which secured a bridge during the Allied advance across Europe. (The action took place at Louvain, in Belgium, by amazing coincidence Corporal Thompson's second Christian name: his father had received news of the birth of his son while passing through the town during the First World War, also serving with the Regiment.)

In 1964 Hanbury's son, 2nd Lieutenant Simon Hanbury, was serving with A Squadron in Cyprus as part of the United Nations Peace-Keeping Force. One of his soldiers drew his attention to a comic that he had been reading: on the front was a pictorial account of the action which portrayed his father, in real life a slim and smart officer, as a cross between Superman and Sapper's Bulldog Drummond!

Berlin was a pleasant posting, though the guard duties, on everything from the Commander in Chief, when in residence, and the GOC British Forces in Berlin, down to coal depots, were heavy. At one point the Regiment provided an escort of eight armoured cars, commanded by Captain Christopher Petherick, for the French commander, General de Beauchesne, when he relinquished his command. On another occasion a Guard was required for Field Marshal

Montgomery. Lieutenant Johnny Wallace was detailed to be the officer, to be replaced shortly before the event when it became known that 'Monty', himself a short man, preferred those guarding him to be of similar size. Lieutenant Dickie Powell was chosen instead.

Off duty there were tours of the shattered city, sailing on the Wannsee, swimming and sunbathing at the Olympic Stadium and the usual soccer, hockey and cricket matches, both inter-squadron and against other formations. There was even a gymkhana held in barracks at Easter, during which Regimental Corporal Major 'Alfie' Hyland came second in the Open Jumping. For those who preferred more sophisticated pursuits, the delights of the Embassy, Bristol and Marlborough clubs provided them. By now there was also a good deal of fraternizing.

This idyllic life was not to continue for long as the Regiment were sent to Luneburg in early June, less one squadron who were to remain for a time in Berlin under the command of 5th Guards Brigade. 2nd Lieutenant Tony Royle, a member of that squadron, remembers that one of their duties was to guard Spandau prison, which was where those Germans eventually convicted of War Crimes charges were to be held.

During what was to be a very brief stay at Luneburg a detachment, consisting of Major Ferris St. George, Squadron Corporal Major Ring, Corporals of Horse Roberts and Hopwood and Troopers Robinson and Martin, went back to England to represent the Regiment on the Victory Parade in London. No sooner was Major St. George back than he was sent off by air in charge of the advance party to Egypt as the Regiment had been warned at short notice for duty in neighbouring Palestine. At that time the country was being governed by the British with the authority of the 1923 League of Nations' Mandate. Riots were also threatened in Cairo and Alexandria.

In all, the Regiment was at Luneburg, under command of 6th Guards Brigade, for a short month. As well as preparing to embark for the Middle East there was extensive patrolling to be done and numerous guard duties in the town itself. The 'Black Market', the name given to the illegal trade in food and goods that were rationed, or otherwise in short supply, had become almost an industry in Germany (it was not unknown in England either at the time). Road-blocks set by A Squadron on the Hamburg-Bremen autobahn yielded a haul of fifty arrests and the confiscation of over thirty tons of contraband.

Finally the Regiment, less those officers and men who were due for release within the next six months, climbed aboard a special train en route for Calais. At Krefeld they were glad to see many of The Blues who had travelled a considerable distance from their Menden base outside the Ruhr in order to greet them. After changing trains at Calais, where the transit camp was not expecting them, it was down to Toulon where, on 9 July, 1946, they embarked on the troopship *Empire Battleaxe* and sailed the same night for Alexandria, together with their 150 tons of equipment.

Five days later they disembarked in the blazing mid-July heat, still dressed in their serge battle-dress more suited to temperate climes, and after a short stay in Amiriya Transit Camp, moved to Kassassin, scene of the Regiment's famous moonlight charge in 1882. Here the Regiment was issued, not with the Daimler armoured cars to which they were all accustomed, but with Staghounds, and Jeeps in lieu of scout cars.

There was an understandable amount of boasting by veterans of the 1st Regiment about how to tackle driving in the sand. Trooper Arthur Rowlinson had joined them in the Desert in 1942 and remembers them as 'immensely proud, like musketeers... all with moustaches'. Various such soldiers in A Squadron decided to show the 'new boys' how it was done and advanced into the sand in their armoured cars. Nemesis was on hand as, to a vehicle, they bogged down, each requiring a pull from the Squadron's REME detachment's recovery vehicle to extricate them.

Lieutenant Colonel Wignall had contracted jaundice shortly before the Regiment's departure from Germany, so Major St. George had assumed temporary command. He felt obliged, in view of the number of men left behind awaiting discharge, to disband D Squadron in order to bring the rest up to strength. The Regiment then moved back to Amiriya, where they trained with the 2nd Royal Irish Fusiliers, for Internal Security duties in Alexandria, should the need arise.

There had been British troops in Egypt for some sixty years, primarily to deter any threat to the Suez Canal, an Anglo-French undertaking that had been opened in 1869. Although Egypt's nominal ruler, King Farouk, was weak and malleable, he found himself swept along with the post-war wave of Arab nationalism: riots against the British presence were on the increase, and in fact the British were in the process of evacuating Cairo and the Nile Delta and concentrating in the area of the Suez Canal, hence the 'Canal Zone'.

Anyway, Acting Lieutenant Colonel Ferris St. George, who had been there with the 1st Regiment in the war, was able to organize expeditions to the nearby battlefield of El Alamein. In 1942, the Regiment had been deep in the desert on the left flank of General Bernard Montgomery's victorious 8th Army during the battle.

Trooper Joseph Douglas, the Troop Leader's driver/mechanic in 3 Troop, A Squadron, remembers how, when on exercise 'in the middle of nowhere', his officer suddenly elected to find the armoured car which he had had to abandon in the North West desert campaign. Douglas, who freely admits that, at the time, he doubted whether any officer could even find the Mediterranean Sea by using a map, let alone a dot in the desert, was much impressed when, two hours later, they found the car, mainly by the use of compass bearings.

Douglas was also one of the few to climb the Great Pyramid, somewhat against his will, he recalls. Sweating along behind the mandatory guide and with an increasing sense of vertigo the higher they climbed, he felt somewhat let down when, on reaching the summit, he found an old Arab selling tea.

In October C Squadron, under the command of Major Muir Turnbull, were dispatched to Cairo to protect British interests from rioting Egyptians, mainly students. Their arrival unhappily coincided with the start of the university term. However, the state of unrest was such that, after only six days, the university was closed and all the potential trouble-makers were sent on vacation. The squadron, which was to be relieved by Major Derek Cooper's B Squadron two months later and then in turn by Major John Greenish's A Squadron, was stationed in the comparative comfort of Kasr-el-Nil barracks (today the Hilton Hotel). One of the main problems there was erecting the Regimental flag on the thirty-foot radio mast; one of the delights was the presence of ATS (Auxiliary Territorial Service), at that time the precursors of the WRAC.

Having just finished fighting in a world war, the concept of 'minimum force', the basis for all Internal Security operations, was alien to the soldiers, indeed to most of the officers as well. All the cars were 'electrified' so as to give a sharp shock to anyone trying to climb on to them while the system was turned on. One of the soldiers' amusements was to leave coins on the sides of the vehicles and watch the temporary distress caused to the occasional light-fingered native. The squadron also provided two troops, commanded by Lieutenants Colin Frost and Jan Barnes, to escort the Chief of the Imperial General Staff through Cairo on his visit to the Middle East.

With Christmas approaching, the annual debate started as to the selection of a suitable Christmas card and, being in the proximity, a copy of the Regimental picture of the Moonlight Charge at the Battle of Kassassin was deemed appropriate. In deference to King

Farouk, the picture was cut out from his copy, but his portly figure was observed in the Union Club at Alexandria taking a deep interest in their 'unexpurgated' copy.

Poor Farouk suffered a further put-down at around the same time when he met Major Turnbull at some social event. ' How long,' asked the King, 'would it take the Regiment, once they had moved to the Canal Zone, to re-enter Cairo?'

'About eight hours,' replied Turnbull.

'And if the Egyptian Army opposed you?' asked Farouk.

'About eight hours and twenty minutes,' replied Turnbull tactlessly, but automatically reflecting the current poor opinion that the British soldiers had of Egypt's finest. The King left the party early.

Before Christmas the Regiment were re-equipped with the familiar Daimler armoured cars (and with Dingo scout cars). The Daimler, with its 2-pounder gun and coaxially mounted Besa medium machine-gun, and the open-topped Dingo with its limited-traverse Bren, were only light reconnaissance vehicles, but were quite fast and manoeuvrable, and ideal for rural Internal Security (IS) work.

Christmas brought a tinge of sadness in that Colonel Wignall, who had been unable to rejoin the Regiment until December, was almost immediately readmitted to hospital and was subsequently medically discharged from the Army, Lieutenant Colonel St. George being confirmed in the appointment as Commanding Officer. Colonel Wignall was able, however, to hang the brick in 1946, having performed the ceremony on the previous Christmas, the first occasion since the war.

'Brick-hanging' is a custom unique to the Warrant Officers' and Corporals' of Horse Mess of The Life Guards, though there have been some crude attempts by other regiments in recent years to emulate it. It originated in 1888 when the Foragemaster of the 2nd Life Guards, one Joe Holland, threw a house-brick onto the forage barn roof before the Christmas break. Once the brick has been hung from the ceiling of the Mess bar, normally about two days before Christmas, thereafter only essential duties are carried out throughout the barracks or camp, until the brick comes down a few days later. Usually the senior retired Regimental Corporal Major performs the task, but provisions were made in the rules for the Commanding Officer to act in lieu if required. Officers, except Commanding Officers when required for the duty, are excluded, though it is an unpopular officer who is not invited into the Mess for a festive drink or three once the brick is 'well and truly hung'.

Christmas was as enjoyable as a group of several hundred fit young men leading a monastic existence in a tented camp a long way from home could make it. In addition to Headquarter Squadron's hilarious production of *Cinderella thro' the Looking Glass*, scripted by Trooper David Cobb, certain privileged ranks were fortunate enough to witness a real pantomime. Corporal of Horse Eric Lloyd, the Sheriff, demanded to see the Identity Card of one Brigadier Foote VC who was on an official visit from the Royal Armoured Corps branch at General Headquarters. 'The officer became rather cross,' recalls Lloyd, adding that the Adjutant, Captain David Hodson, had put him up to it.

In January,1947, the Regiment moved into a hutted camp – a great luxury after six months under canvas – and at the end of March were the last British troops to leave Cairo to join the rest of the Army in Egypt in the Canal Zone. Their new camp at Fanara, about thirty miles north of Suez, was by chance only a few hundred yards from Fayid where the 1st Regiment spent Christmas 1943.

The journey to the new camp was not without a touch of humour from A Squadron. Trooper George Hardy recalls that the vanguard under Major John Greenish (doubtless with the base of his pistol holster tied to his thigh, Wild West fashion, as was his custom) became split. The front part therefore pulled off the road to wait for the second half to catch up. This eventually came into sight, with Lieutenant Jeremy Tree bringing up the rear in his newly-acquired Singer sports car. The lead car saw the other group and slowed down quickly. Tree waved and did not slow down.The ensuing collision did the sports car no good at all. Tree, miraculously unhurt, let loose such a torrent of invective that Trooper Hardy said that he realized for the first time the true meaning of 'to swear like a trooper'.

Hardy himself made a footnote to regimental history later on by becoming the first and only Life Guard to be married in the Middle East on that tour of duty. His wife, Joan, was a clerk in the ATS, and they arranged to marry on 15 May at the church of St Martin-in-the-Sands with The Life Guards' Padre, Rev. HG Taylor, officiating.

Subsequent orders came through for his squadron to move to Palestine on 14 May, 1947, but the service went ahead. Major Greenish told him to 'get the whole thing over as quickly as possible, and get back to the squadron'. However, the Colonel lent his staff car to take the happy couple to a hotel in Cairo for a few days of honeymoon. Fate decreed otherwise, as rioters burned the hotel to the ground that morning. Trooper and Mrs Hardy's first night was postponed for ten months!

Before the move to Palestine took place B Squadron was disbanded owing to lack of manpower, leaving only two Sabre Squadrons, A and

C. This strange anomaly (conscription, introduced at the end of the war, had recently been raised from eighteen months to two years) was due to the lengthy spells of leave under the 'Python' or 'Liap' schemes for those who had been deprived of leave during the war. This meant that at any one time the Regiment would be about sixty men short of their established figure.

Life in Fanara was not amusing: the area was so cramped that any realistic training was out of the question. Sport, too, suffered. Captain and Adjutant David Hodson, writing in the *Household Brigade Magazine*, laconically noted that 'the sports facilities are bad'. The Regiment was kept busy in training the 2nd East Yorks to drive armoured cars, and in patrolling the Alexandria — Cairo road to prevent the natives stealing the telephone cable. Corporal Munn's patrol from A Squadron caught three such thieves who were, Hodson writes, 'duly chastised'.

Also 'duly chastised' if one could catch them were the pickpockets that abounded in the towns. They were usually small boys who worked in gangs and their most popular target was a soldier's pay-book (AB 64) in which he normally carried his weekly pay.

Finally, ten months after they had arrived in the Middle East, ostensibly for duty in Palestine, the order came and the Regiment, led by A Squadron, reached their destination.

Many soldiers from this time have commented on the poor state of the vehicles with which the Regiment were issued. Trooper Douglas in particular remarked that, if it had come to a battle, it would have been encouraging to have armoured cars which would be capable of getting to the battlefield, and hopefully back again, without breaking down on the way. These, and other adverse comments, must be viewed against the fact that all the vehicles were produced against the clock during the war, and many of them were crewed by inexperienced conscripts.

Chapter 2

Palestine (1947-1948)

THE situation in Palestine was fast degenerating by the time that The Life Guards arrived. After General Allenby, aided by T.E. Lawrence (of Arabia) and various Arab forces, drove out the Turks in 1917, the British government, having 'carved up' the Middle East with the French at the secret Sykes-Picot agreement in 1916, were happy to accept the League of Nations' Mandate to govern the country. Nor were the inhabitants, mainly Arab but with a Jewish minority, that displeased to have Ottoman rule replaced by *Pax Britannica*.

The slight hitch was that in 1917 the British Foreign Secretary, A.J. Balfour, had promised in a declaration that was written in to the terms of the Mandate that the Jews could have Palestine as their national homeland, with the condition that it did not prejudice the rights of the existing indigenous population. The Jews, originally from Mesopotamia, had settled in the country after their Exodus from Egypt in the twelfth century BC and had remained there, with various ups and downs, until the Diaspora in 70 AD. The Roman Emperor, Vespasian, had finally lost patience with his ungrateful Jews and ejected or put them to the sword, while his son, the future Emperor Titus, sacked the Temple in Jerusalem.

The Arabs were less than enthusiastic at the Balfour Declaration, but did not react too violently as, initially, there was no rush of Jews to the 'promised land'. Most of them had settled more or less contentedly around the world, particularly in Europe and the United States. However the anti-Jewish attitudes of Hitler's Germany in the 'thirties, which preceded the attempts to expel the race with the *Endlösung*, turned the trickle of immigrants into a deluge.

British attempts to check this flood, and thus pacify the Arabs (oil had been found in many Arab countries), were largely ineffective and pleased neither side. It became clear that Britain would leave, handing the Mandate back to the League of Nations' successor, the United Nations.

The Life Guards, in common with what was, in effect, an army of occupation, found themselves as the meat in the sandwich between the Arabs, who were confident that they could sweep the Jews into the sea when the British had left, and the Jews, who were equally determined that they would stay.

The Arabs therefore contented themselves with attacking Jews if a tempting target was on offer, petty thieving from, and the occasional murder of, British soldiers and fortifying their villages. There was considerable plotting among the Arab states as to who was to command the invasion forces.

However, the Jewish Agency, the Jews' government in waiting, had a defence force, the Haganah, to which most of their able men belonged, many of whom were former British servicemen. Their *corps d'élite* was the Palmach. In addition there were two terrorist murder gangs, the Irgun Zwei Leumi (IZL) of which Menachem Begin, later to be Prime Minster, was a prominent member, and the even more extreme Stern Gang, which contained another future Prime Minister, Yizhak Shamir. These last two groups were independent of each other, but operated together, and indeed with the Palmach and the Haganah when it suited them.

Their object, in which they were highly successful in the short term, was two-fold: to make life so unpleasant for the war-weary British that they would surrender the Mandate and leave, and also to terrorize the Palestinian Arabs so that they too would leave. To this end, they blew up the King David Hotel in 1946 (ninety-one Jews, Arabs and British killed); later massacred eight soldiers of the Parachute Regiment in Tel Aviv; and hanged two British sergeants, booby-trapping one of the bodies, in reprisal for the execution of Dov Grüner, a terrorist. These, and other similar acts, were just for starters: their worst atrocity was perhaps the slaughter of the Arab inhabitants of the village of Deir Yassin. The stupidest was the assassination by the Stern Gang in September, 1948, of the United Nations' mediator, Count Folke Bernadotte, a man of peace. Shamir was also implicated in the assassination of the British minister for the Middle East, Lord Moyne, in Cairo.

That is not to say that the terrorists had it all their own way. Counter-terrorist groups were formed within the Palestine Police, a British-officered force with largely Arab rank and file. Lieutenant Tony Royle recalls meeting Major Roy Farran, a highly decorated former Special Air Service (SAS) officer, seconded to the Police, whose tough team and unusual methods terrorized the terrorists. Farran himself was too well guarded to be murdered. However, his brother was killed with a parcel bomb intended for himself, and there was an attempt to 'frame' him with the murder of a Jewish youth.

To begin with the soldiers were reasonably open minded and did not take the side of either Arab or Jew. Indeed it is doubtful if they really cared who was to gain control of this Holy Land. If anything, for those of the Regiment who had visited Belsen two years before, their sympathies might have been with the Jews, but, as they gained first-hand experience of the Jewish terrorism, such benevolence evaporated. Towards the end the inter-communal atrocities on both sides were so violent that there seemed little to choose between either side.

The Life Guards' first camp, another tented one, was at Khassa, a few miles inland from the Mediterranean and about half way between Gaza and Tel Aviv. The Regiment were under the direct command of the 1st Armoured Division and their duties were primarily in escorts, patrols and guarding themselves. A battalion of Irish Guards were next to them which provided quite an amount of competition on the sports field. Captain Michael Naylor-Leyland, when he arrived from Mounted Duty to join A Squadron, was invited to procure some Arab horses and, with some hounds that another officer somehow produced, they indulged in some jackal hunting, and a little polo as well.

Major John Greenish was determined that his men should not become too bored by being all confined to camp where, sport apart, the only other activity was 'Egyptian PT'. He was apparently a great 'swanner' and would disappear with the complete squadron, either into the Negev desert, or down to the Dead Sea, or across into Jordan. On one of these swans Naylor-Leyland met an old friend serving in the Trans-Jordan Frontier Force in Tiberias. After dining with him he contracted amoebic dysentery and spent the best part of a month in hospital.

Trooper Joseph Douglas, who left school at fourteen to work in a factory and is now a highly qualified mechanical engineer in Florida, kept a diary during the period. Although critical at times of his officers, he gives an insight into conditions prevalent at the time:

24 June, 1947. Quite peeved. Finally, to ease the burden of guard duties and patrols, HQ finally had to lose a night's sleep. On their first patrol [commanded by 2nd Lieutenant Peter Baillie] the blighters apparently hit the jackpot and captured a bunch of dope smugglers. The loot was apparently worth about £4,000 and a $1,000 bribe was offered. ... Life was so unfair... that they were the lucky ones to have a bit of excitement first time out.

30 June. 7.30pm. A report came through that a ship suspected of gun-running was waiting to slip ashore under cover of

1. Nijmegen, Holland, Spring, 1945. Cpl (later RCM) Eric Lloyd with Tprs Moore, Gosling, Randall and Barker. (*John Randall*)

2. The Brandenburg Gate, Berlin, in 1946. (*David Palmer*)

3. The Dry Roger: acquired in 1945.

5. The route home: Hanover station in 1946. (*John Randall*)

4. At the foot of King Farouk's statue, Alexandria, Egypt, 1947: *back row* Tprs Kaiser, Chance. *Front ro* Cpl Clarke, Tprs Webster, Wilson. (*M Webster*)

6. Tpr Robinson at the wheel of Cpl Dart's Dingo 'Amok', Palestine 1948. (*J March*)

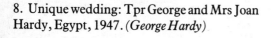

7. After the hijack: Cpl Dart's Dingo showing the entry point of the AP shot. (*David Palmer*)

8. Unique wedding: Tpr George and Mrs Joan Hardy, Egypt, 1947. (*George Hardy*)

9. Capt Michael Naylor-Leyland MC (*Navana Vandyk*)

10. The newly commissioned 2Lt Michael Wyndham, 1948. (*Hay Wrightson*)

11. Lt Mike Thomas with the Guard, Windsor Castle, 1948. Tpr Eric Morris is in the rear rank, third from the right. (*Geo Spearman*)

darkness. We dashed down to the coast and the two scout cars set up an OP (Observation Post) ... but nothing happened.

10 July. Drove scout car as escort for field cashier supposed to be carrying £20,000. ... He drove as if the devil were behind him. ... A jeep with two Military Police tried to flag us down but, fortunately for them, they backed off. ... I would have been quite happy to have pushed them [off the road] at top speed.

2 October.12.45 am. Came off guard with one and a quarter hours' sleep and drove a Daimler armoured car in convoy to Lake Tiberias over 100 miles of mountain passes, dead tired. The thought of the sheer drop of hundreds of feet to the valley on my right kept me awake.

During the period the Colonel broke his jaw playing polo at Sarafand and was away for four months. His replacement during his enforced absence was Major W.H. Gerard Leigh, or G as he was generally known to his brother officers. Although pleased to be offered command, albeit temporary, at the age of thirty-two, (he was to command again in 1953), G, who had graduated through Staff College at the end of the war, had recently married and had a comfortable Staff appointment as DAAG (Discipline) at Headquarters, London District. He was therefore less than pleased. He had been in Palestine in 1940 with the 1st Regiment and their horses and, as an officer who had attended the long equitation course at Weedon, had been temporarily attached to the cavalry school in Palestine at the time. Now there was not a great deal going on in the country to speak of, and he was enjoying married life in London.

He was even more disgruntled when Colonel Ferris St. George returned to duty, as the AG17 branch in Egypt, having, as they saw it, expended something in the region of £70 to get G out to the Middle East, were reluctant to repeat the expenditure to book him a berth home so soon. When he eventually offered to pay for the passage himself, the authorities relented and he was allowed home to take command of the mounted squadron at Knightsbridge.

Meanwhile, the record recalls, Captain David Hodson, Orderly Room Quartermaster Corporal (Chief Clerk) Dennis Meakin and Corporal of Horse Eric Lloyd were among those who departed temporarily on their six-month Python leave. Captain David Palmer became Adjutant, Captains Paddy Drummond and John Gemmell became acting squadron leaders and for a time Lieutenant Hon. Robin Borwick became Chief Clerk, the first and last time that an officer was to hold the post. They were all under the age of twenty-one.

Trooper Douglas and two other Life Guards took a week's local leave to Cyprus, then a colony. From the leave centre on the beach at Famagusta they went exploring, only to find themselves outside a building with a large sign proclaiming it to be 'Taverne-am-Meer', and surrounded by Germans! They had walked into a POW camp with no guards in sight. Since the three friends had all fought in the war, the experience was initially strange, but they were made to feel very welcome and plied with Cypriot wine. 'We were soon overwhelmed by these poor fellows, anxious for any information from home,' wrote Douglas. 'We tried, in our basic German, to let them know what was going on without hurting anyone's feelings.'

In October two troops from A Squadron were detached for duties in support of the Police in Jerusalem, a commitment later to be taken on by C Squadron. In November the United Nations voted in favour of the establishment of a Jewish State in Palestine. In December Lieutenant Victor Hoare and Squadron Corporal Major Cookson, while visiting the detachment in Jerusalem, were both shot in the back at point-blank range by IZL gunmen. They were both severely wounded but survived. The terrorists, unusually, justified the act by saying that the attack was in response to a previous assault on a Jewish girl by (unspecified) soldiers, rather a loose interpretation of 'an eye for an eye'.

Major Muir Turnbull, with a party of C Squadron and Royal Artillery, was, for a time, sent around the villages in an early effort at winning 'hearts and minds'. He was reasonably welcomed in the Arab villages, once it had been established that they were not Jews in stolen uniforms. He also had to provide a strong escort to take about forty terrorists from Acre to Jerusalem. 'None escaped,' wrote Turnbull, recalling that they were all chained together by the ankles for the journey.

C Squadron were also responsible, during their time in Jerusalem, for escorting convoys of old and slow lorries from the Palestine Potash Company near Jericho up to Jerusalem. The rocky terrain was ideal for ambushes, and all the troops in the squadron had some action in dealing with them while involved in convoy protection. A particularly hot spot was for the troops who did the daily run down the road adjoining the Old City Wall; fire was drawn from not only Arab and Jew, but also, Turnbull suspects, from the bored soldiers of the British battalion in Notre Dame Barracks opposite the Jaffa Gate!

Towards the end of February, 1948, C Squadron were replaced in Jerusalem by A Squadron, who were billeted with a battalion of the Warwickshire Regiment, while Regimental Headquarters and Headquarter Squadron were based with the garrison at Sarafand. C

Squadron moved south of Gaza and joined 2nd King's Royal Rifle Corps in preparation for the British withdrawal when the Mandate ended on 15 May. The luckless Commanding Officer no sooner had returned to duty after his polo accident than he badly sprained his ankle, it is alleged by playing passage football in the Mess.

The final few weeks of the Mandate were, for the Regiment, literally action-packed. Corporal of Horse Jenkins, for instance, had the ignominy of being captured, together with his troop, by Arabs and held prisoner for a time in a cave near Bethlehem. Other incidents were plentiful, three, however, are brought up time and again, and are perhaps typical examples.

The first was the kidnapping of Corporal Jimmy Dart and his driver, Trooper Robinson and the highjacking of their Dingo scout car by Jewish Irregulars. The pair were part of a half-troop patrol (one Daimler, one Dingo) from 1 Troop, A Squadron, which was returning to their base near the Jewish Agency building in King George V Avenue, Jerusalem. They were coming back from a run twenty-five miles down the Jaffa road when Corporal John March's Daimler developed intermittent engine trouble. March, who was commanding the patrol, ordered Corporal Dart to go on ahead and rendezvous with him later on the outskirts of the City. This order was a mistake, as armoured car patrols should not be split down to less than two. A pair of cars can give each other supporting fire when needed, single cars can not.

As March's car coughed and spluttered around one of the last bends in the hills around the City, they came upon the Dingo, halted at a road-block of oil drums and rocks, minus its crew and surrounded by armed civilians. There was no question of driving round the block; there was a drop to the left and hillside to the right and the crowd were gesturing with Thompson sub-machine guns. March ordered his driver to 'put his foot down' and the Daimler crashed through the obstacles, coming under small arms fire as it did. A terrorist leaped on the (rear) engine deck, so they closed the turret hatch and 'a quick traverse of the turret soon dismounted him' as March put it.

They halted a few hundred yards further on, turned round and cautiously moved back to the scene. When rounding the last bend they saw two terrorists jump into the scout car and start to drive it off up a side track. Trooper J. Mulgrew, March's gunner/signaller, needed no orders. He rammed an armour-piercing shell into the breech of the 2-pounder, while March called up over the wireless for permission to open fire. This granted, Mulgrew took aim and fired.

The Dingo rolled back on to the road and one man jumped out,

17

removing the Bren gun as he did. March, mindful of the fact that a Daimler had been stolen at gun-point earlier from a garage where it was undergoing repairs, ordered Mulgrew to open fire with the Besa machine gun on a suspicious green vehicle behind some bushes, and drove back to the Dingo. Both Major Hall and Captain Naylor-Leyland remember that March had left the pressel switch on his hand-set on 'send', so the whole squadron wireless net was treated to a broadcast of the shot being fired, and the whoop of glee as the target was struck.

Mulgrew's shot had entered through the louvres at the back of the engine compartment, passed through the engine's rocker-box, thence into the back of the fighting compartment where it made a considerable mess of the 19-set wireless, and of the Jewish driver. The 'armoured car' in the bushes turned out to be a milk lorry, leaking copiously!

Major Tony Hall, A Squadron Leader, had been aloft at the time in an Auster spotter 'plane. He immediately contacted the local branch of the Haganah at the Jewish Agency and ordered them to effect the release of Dart and Robinson. He threatened that, if that was not forthcoming, the entire squadron would line up before the flats to which he thought that they had been taken, and would open fire. This fine example of 'gunboat diplomacy' worked and the two men were handed back unharmed. In return the Jewish Agency were allowed to retrieve their dead comrade and were further invited to clean up the interior of the Dingo.*

The second incident concerned the ambush by Arabs of a Jewish supply convoy at the Arab village of Sheikh Jarrah on 13 April, 1948. The village lay astride the only route to the Hadassah Hospital and the Hebrew University on Mount Scopus. Although there had been a tacit agreement in the past to allow these convoys safe passage, the Arabs on this occasion were apparently inflamed at the news of the massacre at Deir Yassin three days before. At around half past nine they blew the road in front of the convoy's leading armoured car which brought the column to a halt.

The explosion was heard in the Old City, and soon Arabs were

---

* Memories have faded somewhat over the years, and as a result there are several versions of this tale. What is reasonably beyond doubt is that a Daimler had been stolen earlier from A Squadron. It was never recovered, despite the efforts of Captain Naylor-Leyland, who even persuaded the Haganah to allow him into one of their camps to show him that they had not got the vehicle. They had it, of course, and Trooper Eric Morris saw it at the head of a Haganah parade on an old newsreel clip shown on television some years ago. The main account of Corporal Dart's Dingo is based on the written evidence of Corporal March and Trooper Morris.

flocking to the scene to join their comrades in the slaughter that followed. Sheikh Jarrah lay in an area for which the Highland Light Infantry had responsibility and the battalion's second in command, Major Jack Churchill, was quickly on hand to make an appreciation of the situation. He called up Jerusalem Command to ask for a half-troop of armoured cars, an Artillery Observation Officer, and for permission to use his mortars. The last two requests were denied, and when the half-troop of Life Guards from A Squadron arrived, it became obvious that a larger force was needed.

Accordingly Captain Michael Naylor-Leyland took charge of three troops and they drove to Sheikh Jarrah. In conjunction with Major Churchill, Naylor-Leyland made a plan whereby the infantry would provide cover for his men to evacuate the survivors. He fired off the smoke grenade dischargers with which every armoured car was fitted in order to provide a smoke-screen; however, that was insufficient so he had to call Squadron Corporal Major Radcliffe, who was manning the radio net, to ask the artillery for smoke from their 25-pounder guns. There was some delay up the line, as his request came back with a query as to what sort of smoke he wanted, but eventually it was forthcoming.

Naylor-Leyland and his Life Guards looped around the convoy with difficulty (it was pinned down in a built-up area and some vehicles were ablaze) and, under small-arms fire, evacuated the survivors and the wounded, using some of the armoured engine-decks as shields. At one point he was obliged to use the 2-pounder main armament of his Daimler, which was against the local rules of engagement, to silence a fierce and accurate Arab source of fire which was threatening his men. The HLI, not noted for their timidity, had an unusually hard time with the Arabs who, for once, were so determined to destroy the Jews to a man that close-quarter fighting ensued.

Finally the action ended. The Jews had lost about seventy-six dead, many of them doctors and scholars. By good fortune The Life Guards had sustained no casualties. Captain Naylor-Leyland was later awarded the Military Cross for his part in relieving the column.

The final major action for The Life Guards came on 25 April, 1948. With the end of the Mandate only three weeks away, the Jews were trying to seize towns, as well as villages. Tiberias, Haifa, Safed and Cabala all fell to their forces. Stung by Arab criticism that the British forces were sitting placidly by, Foreign Secretary Ernest Bevin ordered General Sir Gordon MacMillan, GOC Palestine, to stop the Jews from capturing the port of Jaffa from the Arabs.

Regimental Headquarters had always maintained a duty troop,

manned on a rotating basis by RHQ and HQ Squadron personnel at Sarafand. On this occasion it was commanded by Captain David Palmer. Major Derek Cooper, who had originally transferred from the Irish Guards and was Second in Command of the Regiment, took command of a force which also had another troop, commanded by 2nd Lieutenant Digby Neave from C Squadron, a troop of tanks from the 4th/7th Dragoon Guards (later their troop leader, 2nd Lieutenant Robin Huntingdon was awarded the Military Cross) and infantry from the Royal Irish Fusiliers. In support he had artillery, aircraft and naval gun-fire.

When he entered the town, the centre was under heavy mortar fire from a large force of Haganah, Palmach, IZL and the Stern Gang, and there were many civilian casualties. The line to the north of the port was being held with increasing difficulty by ex-Palestine Police Arabs and some Iraqi irregulars. Cooper's force advanced through this line, and for the next five days there was heavy house-to-house fighting, a scout car being knocked out, a tank being damaged and the infantry sustaining casualties.

David Ben Gurion, soon to be Prime Minister of the new state of Israel, then called for a cease-fire so that the wounded could be evacuated. This was broken on the following day with a heavy mortar attack from the IZL, so the fighting continued, accompanied with loud-speaker exhortations to the Arabs to 'Get out with the British and remember Deir Yassin!'. This the Arabs did, for when the British withdrew from Jaffa on 10 May, leaving an estimated 500 Jewish casualties, with Arabs clinging to the sides of their vehicles, 65,000 out of a total population of 70,000 had fled. Major Cooper, who received a Military Cross for his part in the action, has been involved in relief work for Palestinian refugees in the occupied territories ever since.

The withdrawal from what was now the State of Israel took place over 15/16 May, 1948, the Regiment driving south across the Sinai desert to Ismailia and maintaining wireless contact throughout on the 19-set wireless. On the way they encountered columns of Egyptian troops streaming towards Israel, and at one point C Squadron were bombed and machine-gunned by a flight of Egyptian Spitfires, Troopers Thacker and Shann being injured. Their ground forces seemed well equipped and disciplined, although it was later established that they had no maps. Also they appeared to be keener on 'liberating' Arab villages rather than 'mixing it' with the very determined Jews in their fortified villages, which they contented themselves with bombarding from a distance. The rest is history.

The Regiment finally came together for the first time in some months and, after a short spell in a transit camp at Port Said, embarked for home on the troopship *Cheshire*, arriving at Liverpool on 6 June, 1948. Before they left the transit camp, however, Major Cooper, and Captain Naylor-Leyland, who is generally held to have been the last soldier out of Jerusalem, made use of letters of introduction to a Minister of the Egyptian government. Later they took his two very attractive daughters out to dinner, thence to an open-air night club on top of the Semiramis Hotel in Cairo. After a time Naylor-Leyland noticed some Arabs having a lively discussion over a map of Palestine (the only one, perhaps). As he put it, he weaved his way over to their table to offer advice, only to be firmly told that ' His Majesty does not require your help'. He had interrupted King Farouk's Orders Group who were working out the casualty lists to date.

The Regiment were greeted on landing at Liverpool, having not served as a regiment in the country for eight years, by Major General the Earl of Athlone (the Colonel of the Regiment), Colonel Sir Henry Abel Smith (the Silver Stick) and Major Gerard Leigh (commanding the mounted squadron).

Chapter 3

Windsor (1948-1952)

A SPECIAL train took The Life Guards from Liverpool to Pirbright, Surrey, a Foot Guard camp, though not at that time the Guards Depot, which was then at Caterham. From there the entire Regiment went on a month's well-earned leave.

Slight consternation greeted them on their return, as Headquarter Squadron and Regimental Headquarters had smuggled back with them from Palestine several tortoises (Captain David Hodson was the 'tortoise officer'), and these had been 'liberated' in the Officers' Mess garden. The dozen or so chelonians had set to with a will on the rich and strange diet of footguard flora, much to the dismay of the gardening officer.

The Regiment then reorganized before moving to Combermere Barracks, Windsor, to take on the role of 'Household Cavalry Basic Regiment', an unwieldy title soon dropped in favour of their own. Prior to the war, The Life Guards and the Royal Horse Guards alternated between London and Windsor and both trained their own recruits to ride in whichever barracks they occupied at the time.

Now there was not only the need to train the regular recruits and some of the older soldiers for mounted duty, and to train all the recruits for the Household Cavalry, both regular and conscripted, in basic training (drill, weapon training, map reading and so forth), but also, for those destined for the two armoured car regiments, in technical training. This involved a six-week course in either driving an armoured car, learning the techniques involved in firing both the main and the coaxial armaments or being instructed in the mysteries of the 19-set wireless (not to be known as 'radio' until the mid-fifties).

There was also the band to administer, a demonstration squadron to run and, if that were not enough, to take over the resident Foot Guard barracks (Victoria) from the 3rd Grenadiers who left at short notice on an emergency posting to Malaya. To crown it all there was a commitment to take on the dismounted guard at Windsor Castle from the Ist Scots Guards!

The Castle Guard commitment for the Regiment only lasted for five months before being relieved by the 1st King's Shropshire Light Infantry. Trooper Eric Morris was a member of the last guard which the Regiment provided, and he remembers the new guard from the Light Infantry arriving at the Castle at their normal march of 120 paces to the minute.

The Regiment were to spend the next three years in Windsor as a training regiment. This was a particularly soul-destroying period. 'There is very little to report on since the last issue' became almost the standard refrain in the Regimental Intelligence section in the quarterly Household Brigade magazine.

Training conscripts has been likened to painting the Firth of Forth railway bridge. To get a raw recruit through General Military Training (GMT) and to get him a basic trade (gunner, driver or signaller) took the best part of six months; and to get him a second trade in order to make him a useful member of an armoured car troop (and thus increase his qualification-related pay) would depend very much on when a vacancy on a course occurred. One then had a reasonably trained, but inexperienced, trooper for around a year before he started to get 'demob-happy' while ticking off the 'days-to-do' on his 'chuff-chart'.

Perhaps, hardly surprisingly, after both a World War and by being out of the country, effectively, for eight years there was a lack of both potential officers and soldiers coming forward for regular engagements; so much so that on occasions the brighter conscripts ended their service as instructors themselves.

'National Service' was the dressed-up name that conscription was given, and it was to continue until 1962. The young men were all caught up in it. To avoid it was firstly impossible except for miners and trawlermen, and secondly it would have been socially unacceptable. In all walks of life young men accepted their lot and made, by and large, good soldiers.

Only one building, the Riding School, survives of the old Combermere Barracks. The sixteen-acre site, Cavalry Barracks to The Blues, Combermere to The Life Guards (Viscount Combermere had been the latter's Colonel), contained a cavalry barracks allegedly designed for India. In the centre was the Officers' House, the lawn of which was flanked by two two-story barrack blocks, K and L. These had barrack rooms sleeping up to thirty men in double-tiered beds on the top two floors and horses in stalls on the ground floor level. The barracks were also rat-infested and two musicians of the band were bitten by rats at around this time.

The walled barracks contained all the usual buildings to be found in a Victorian cavalry barracks: a forge, veterinary lines, forage barns, the barrack field where, in addition to the riding school, equitation was taught, together with the more normal offices, stores, messes and a hospital.

A point to remember is that at that time the only attached personnel to be found with either regiment of Household Cavalry were the Royal Electrical and Mechanical Engineers (REME) craftsmen of the Light Aid Detachment (LAD) and the odd pay clerk from the Royal Army Pay Corps (RAPC). All the cooks, clerks, medical orderlies, farriers, physical training instructors and tailors were fully-fledged members of their regiment, though they naturally received the appropriate training after completing their General Military Training at Windsor.

The Medical Officers and, in Knightsbridge the Veterinary Officer, would originate from the Royal Army Medical Corps (or the Royal Army Veterinary Corps) and thereafter often would spend the rest of their service as part of the Regiment and wear regimental uniform.

This then was the setting for the 'Household Cavalry Basic Regiment'. On paper the establishment looked tiny: a Headquarter Squadron (Major Tony Meredith-Hardy), a Training Squadron (Major Derek Cooper) and a Demonstration Squadron, later to be called D Squadron (Major Peter Herbert). In practice it was so huge that D Squadron, based in Victoria Barracks for the Castle Guard, had to move to Pirbright thereafter. All the technical training, and the soldiers undergoing it, were housed in the Imperial Service College a quarter of a mile away, or at Pirbright.

In addition to the tasks already enumerated the Regiment also had to run summer camps for the Territorial Army (TA). National Servicemen and three-year regular soldiers all had a commitment to join the TA at the end of their service with the result that it was of considerable size. The Household Cavalry was responsible in particular for the Inns of Court and City Yeomanry. Their headquarters were in the City and the Regiments would supply the Second in Command, or Training Major, and Adjutant, together with a number of Non-Commissioned Officers as instructors.

Certificate 'A' boards were another chore. Most schools ran Combined Cadet Forces (CCFs) where the certificates of proficiency were the 'Cert. A parts 1 and 2'. In truth these were rather a confidence trick as, whatever inducements were made at the time about them being 'so useful when you come to do your National Service', in practice they hardly promised a head start when it came to the adult version.

The CCF, successor to the public school OTC, did however give the young men a taste of the discipline to come. The boards themselves would entail half a dozen officers and NCOs spending the best part of a day at some school, private or state, to test the youths in turnout, drill, fieldcraft, weapon handling and map-reading.

Likewise schools in the Windsor area would send parties of their cadets to Combermere Barracks on day visits. Eton College, being just the other side of the Thames, was one of the nearest and that is possibly the reason for the disproportionate amount of Old Etonian officers, and indeed the occasional soldier, who passed through both regiments both in the 'fifties and early 'sixties.

Officers and men obviously were constantly arriving and leaving for their two-year stint of conscription; regulars (the initial engagements were then either seven years with the Colours and five years on the reserve, or six and four) arrived too and were in turn posted in and out, many to the mounted regiment at Knightsbridge.

Since the mounted regiment was formed at the end of the Second World War it has always been the policy, where possible, for officers to do two postings at mounted duty of about two years at a time and for soldiers who seem to be planning to serve for the full twenty-two years to do likewise. Thus any Life Guard approaching Field or Warrant rank will have had experience of both the ceremonial and the mechanized roles.

The winter of 1948 saw the arrival of two young officers who were to add much colour to the regiment over the following two decades: 2nd Lieutenants Viscount (Simon) Galway and Ian Baillie. Their arrival was fairly muted, and after a year they were sent off to The Blues in Germany for three months to gain practical experience.

In the following Spring Captain David Palmer, who was Drill Adjutant at Mons Officer Cadet Training Unit at Aldershot where National Service officers received their brief four-month training, returned for a month to run a young officers' cadre. These events were often quite fun and amusing, and involved as many subalterns as could be gathered together for a fortnight, or longer, drilling each other on the drill square, being lectured to by the senior officers and taking to the field from time to time to deploy notional troops in battle positions.

On one occasion in the late 'fifties Lieutenant Arthur Gooch, who had recently attended a Nuclear, Biological and Chemical (NBC) warfare course, caused the Regimental Corporal Major near apoplexy on one such cadre. He scattered radio-active sources around the square and issued all the young officers with Geiger counters. The object was for the students to plot 'ground zero' from a mythical nuclear explosion. While Life Guards have never held the square in the same awe as do the Foot Guards, the sight of twenty-odd young officers disrupting recruits' drill was almost too much to bear for the Regimental Corporal Major.

On another occasion, in the early 'sixties, the Commanding Officer, Lieutenant Colonel Julian Fane MC, was lecturing his officers on 'Duties in aid of the Civil Power', a favourite military topic at that time. He was citing General Dyer's rather straightforward methods at Amritsar, in the days of the Raj, as an example of how not to break up a riot, when whispering broke out in the audience. General Dyer, so the rumour stated, had been 2nd Lieutenant Peter Bickmore's grandfather. (He hadn't.) This caused great amusement to all except the Colonel.

1949 also saw the arrival of Surgeon Captain Geoffrey Bulow, the return to duty of Corporal Major Cookson, who had been injured after being shot in the back in Palestine, and the arrival of 2nd Lieutenant William Edgedale. Finally at the end of the year Lieutenant Colonel E.J.S. 'Jackie' Ward MC transferred from The Blues to take command, Colonel Ferris St George moving up to become Silver Stick *vice* Colonel Sir Henry Abel Smith DSO.

1949 also saw the complete training schedule disrupted as 400 men were deployed to the London Docks during a dock strike and an additional training commitment of twenty-eight recruits per month for the Royal Armoured Corps.

Riding School Corporal Major Walter Thompson won the King's Cup (showjumping) at the Royal Tournament at Earl's Court in the summer, the first occasion that 'Other Ranks' were allowed to compete, and Father Christmas fell down the chimney!

Every Christmas, wartime apart, a Christmas party is held for all the regimental children. A lavish tea is prepared in the cook-house, an entertainer booked and the high point is the arrival of Santa down the chimney with presents for all the children. For this Christmas Corporal Dunton, the regimental barber, played the part of Santa. Festively clad he climbed through a cook-house window that had been blanked off to resemble a chimney-breast, and started the descent down the suitably positioned ladder to the floor.

Whether Corporal Dunton had over-imbibed with Christmas spirit at lunch-time, or whether, as he said, he slipped does not really matter; he arrived at speed in the mock hearth emitting a volley of unseasonable oaths. 'That's not Father Christmas, it's Mr Dunton,' cried the children, their beliefs, and indeed some of the presents, shattered.

1950 witnessed the arrival of 2nd Lieutenants John Gooch and Desmond Langley, and the return from Knightsbridge of Captain

Naylor-Leyland as Equitation Officer to the Household Cavalry. It also saw the departure for civilian life of Captains David Palmer and Tony Hall, and the resurgence of what the Army is pleased to call 'Equitation'. For this all credit must go to Major Peter Herbert MC for organizing a morning Officers' Ride and persuading Colonel St. George to allow officers to take a day off during the week in order to hunt.

With the requirement for all regular officers to go through riding school, regardless of any previous experience, it followed that many of them acquired a taste for more competitive mounted pursuits. For Captain Henry Montgomerie-Charrington and 2nd Lieutenant David Keith their sport was point-to-pointing; for others it was hunting. Indeed in the following year the officers purchased a horse-box to enable them to hunt regularly with the Grafton whose master, former Life Guard Major Neil Foster and huntsman, Will Pope, provided good sport.

The Regiment was responsible for running the Army Hunter Trials in the autumn and Major Tony Meredith-Hardy was in charge of the event which was held at Stanlake Park near Twyford. A regimental team consisting of Veterinary Major Jack Dalzell, Lieutenant Toni Chiesman and Corporal Major Walter Thompson were placed 2nd.

Through the good offices of a former Carabinier captain, one Eddie Crane*, and the impresario Jack Hilton, a concert was held in April which featured stars of the day such as George Formby. The King, Queen and Princess Margaret attended and later joined the officers for supper, and for dancing to both the regimental band and the Cuban band of Edmundo Ross in the Officers' House.

On a sociological point it is worth mentioning that at around this time the Warrant Officers and Non-Commissioned Officers decided to abandon the serving hatch in their mess through which they were wont to order their drinks. In its place they erected a cocktail bar.

In December, 1950, the King announced that in future the Household Cavalry were formally to join with the Brigade of Guards to form the new Household Brigade. This went some way to regularizing the status of the small corps of Household Cavalry which up till then were fully accepted by neither the Line Cavalry nor the Brigade of Guards. The Regiment now came under the Major General Commanding the Household Brigade (subsequently retitled the

---

* Captain Crane's connection with the Regiment was through the Silver Stick Adjutant, Captain Clary Piff of the Blues. The pair were well known for a time for their elaborate entertaining.

Household Division in 1968), though they continued to be under the Director, Royal Armoured Corps, for technical matters.

Good news arrived at the start of 1951, namely that the Regiment were to give up their onerous training role and re-form as an armoured car regiment prior to being posted to Germany at the start of the following year. No tears were shed when all of the recruits, less those in training for mounted duty at Knightsbridge, moved lock, stock and barrel to 67 Training Regiment, RAC, at Hadrian's Camp, Carlisle, in June.

Later in the year Captain Naylor-Leyland, who had earlier won the Royal Artillery one-day event, was told that he had been officially selected for the three-day event team for the 1952 Olympics. This recalled the 1948 Olympics prior to which he had rashly made a suggestion before lunch at Knightsbridge. This was that any reasonably fit man should be capable of completing the marathon within four hours. This was due to be run from the Copper Horse in Windsor Great Park to Wembley Stadium.

Wagers were made on the basis that he could not complete a similar course between Combermere and Knightsbridge in the stipulated time. The odds came down from 6-1 to 4-1, so Naylor-Leyland decided two days later to try a training run round Hyde Park. Accompanied by Lieutenant Duncan Llewellyn he set off, but by the time that they had reached Hyde Park Corner (under half way) the pair felt so ill that they took a taxi back to barracks.

Two days later he drove down to Windsor, consumed a large glass of port and two digestive biscuits, and set off in his tennis shoes. Three hours fifty-one minutes later, leaving a trail of blood from his blistered feet along Kensington High Street, he arrived at Knightsbridge. To the subsequent delight of his tailor and others he had won about £800, a considerable sum in those days.

Other mounted successes in 1951 were Corporal Major Thompson's 5th placing at the Badminton three-day event and Corporal Mitchell's double achievement in winning both the King's and Prince of Wales's Cups at the Royal Tournament, as had Thompson in the previous year.

Exercise 'Surprise Packet' in October saw the Regiment deployed on Salisbury Plain and coming under command of both 65th Armoured Brigade and 16th Airborne Division. This was the first time in over three years that the Regiment had been allowed out, so to speak, so each squadron spent a week in training at Pirbright, followed by a further week in the field, before the exercise started.

After Christmas leave the Regiment prepared to move to relieve

The Blues in Germany. 26 February was the planned date of departure, so Rev. Eric Dawson-Walker, the 'Rifting Rector' of the Holy Trinity church in Windsor, the Household Cavalry's adopted spiritual base, held a farewell service on 3 February. On 6 February King George VI died.

Fortunately contingency plans, prepared by the Lord Chamberlain's office and by Headquarters, Household Brigade, exist for such sad but predictable occasions. The first stage was the Proclamation of the new Monarch, Queen Elizabeth II. Escorted by two parties under the command of Captain Llewellyn and Lieutenant Keith, the Mayor of Windsor read the proclamation to the people of Windsor by the statue of Queen Victoria, then to the Dean and the Military Knights in the Castle. From there, he went down the hill to Eton Bridge, the route being lined by two squadrons commanded by Majors Wordsworth and Greenish, to read the proclamation to the people and schoolboys of Eton.

The Commanding Officer commanded the Sovereign's Escort for the State Funeral at Windsor which consisted of two dismounted divisions of Life Guards in khaki, and two mounted divisions, one Life Guard and one of Blues in full dress from the Mounted Regiment. The hardest part of the sad occasion was accommodating the party from London, in addition to 160 sailors and 150 policemen, in Comber-mere.

All of this delayed the departure by a few days, so it was not until 3 March, 1952, that the Regiment marched to Windsor railway station, thence by train to Southampton to embark on the *Charlton Star* for the Hook of Holland. They were joined in time for the voyage by Lieutenant Christopher Phillipson from Knightsbridge and by 2nd Lieutenant Christopher Wordsworth, younger brother of Major Robin. Sadly left behind was Captain Naylor-Leyland, who retired in order to train for the Olympics. His departure as Equitation Officer of the Household Cavalry led to the commissioning into the Regiment of Corporal Major Walter 'Tommy' Thompson who filled the long-vacant post of Riding Master.

Chapter 4

Wolfenbüttel (1952-1954)

TWO days later the Regiment reached Northampton Barracks, Wolfenbüttel, which they found much improved since they had last left them in 1946. Germany was now an 'accompanied' posting, so the wives and families of officers and men lived in quarters near the barracks.

The role that the Regiment was to fill was that of deterring any advance westwards by forces of the Soviet Union and its satellites in Eastern Europe. When it had become plain that the Russian-led forces had no intention of pulling back from the line across Germany that they had reached by the end of the Second World War, the predominantly American and British 'Western Powers' felt obliged to do likewise. In 1949 the North Atlantic Treaty Organization (NATO) mutual defence pact was signed. Now The Life Guards were part of the British Rhine Army guarding the northern half of what Churchill called the 'Iron Curtain' which physically divided the East of Europe from the West.

Before the memories fade it is worth recording that the Iron Curtain, constructed by the Warsaw Pact forces, came to consist of an unbroken line of barbed-wire, mines, watch-towers and armed guards which stretched from the Baltic to the Black Sea. It was designed, as was later the Berlin Wall, more to keep disaffected East Europeans in the East rather than as a defensive measure against possible Western aggression.

The first visitor to the Regiment was Major General H.R.B. Foote VC, in command of the 11th Armoured Division, the Regiment's higher command, and better known in the Regiment as the officer pulled up by Provost Corporal of Horse Lloyd for not producing his Identity Card in Egypt five years earlier. It was either for Foote or for some other VIP that all ranks were ordered to remove their khaki caps and give three cheers, an unusual practice.

It was a prevalent offence at that time for the soldiers to unpick the stitching that held the peaks to their caps. They all did, of course, because the caps were issued in the shape of postmen's caps and the object was to rearrange the cap and peak in such a way that they were both near to the vertical. Therefore when the order was given for the three cheers, a certain amount of peakless khaki caps flew through the air. Trooper Kenneth Rowden, who had achieved brief fame at Windsor for bayoneting the Orderly Officer, thought to have been Lieutenant Simon Sainsbury, in the smog on night-guard (they both lived!) remembers that 'the officers and NCOs appeared to be upset; a touchy lot I thought.'

Rowden also took part in 'The Great Tram Ride'. Soon after the Regiment's arrival in Wolfenbüttel a group of Life Guards decided to sample the ale in nearby Brunswick. None of them had cars in those days, but Germany was well covered by an electric tram service, and it was by tram that they made their way to Brunswick.

It was most probably the evening of Pay Day (soldiers were paid weekly in cash until the early 'seventies) because the town was thick with the loathed Military Police on their town patrols. All soldiers were, of course, easily identifiable as they had to be in uniform.

Anyway, an evening of fraternizing and drinking behind them, in high good humour Rowden and his friends boarded a tram to take them back to barracks in Wolfenbüttel, some seven miles distant. Someone suggested that Life Guards should be in charge. The German driver in his peaked cap initially demurred, but later surrendered the controls to this bunch of huge soldiers. (Five foot eight inches was the lower height limit for the Household Cavalry, at that time well above the average national height for both Britain and Germany.)

Rowden did not, so far as he remembers, take charge of the tram himself, but remembers the 'fixed glazed smiles' on the faces of the German passengers as the tram passed all of the many halts without stopping to let passengers on or off. There was quite a reception committee waiting for them at the Wolfenbüttel terminus, but, since no one had been offered violence and no damage had been done, the men got off lightly.

The Regiment had been reorganized into the standard three Sabre Squadron establishment (A, C and D to be different). Each squadron itself had five sabre troops, each of two Daimler armoured cars and two Dingo scout cars, a 6 (Assault) Troop in White scout cars and a 7 (Heavy) Troop with four AEC armoured cars. The .38 revolver and the Sten-gun were the standard personal weapons for, respectively, officers and men, while the assault troopers had the faithful .303 Lee-Enfield rifle. The Bren-gun was the Dingo's only armament; however, all of the 'A' (fighting) vehicles were fitted with multiple smoke grenade dischargers.

The first priority, though, was communications, so some 'Wireless Schemes' were held before the later 'Tactical Exercises without

Troops' (TEWTs) exercised the squadron and Regimental Headquarter elements. A quick succession of manoeuvres followed with names like 'Red Patch' and 'Lawnmower'. For the final exercise of the year, the Regiment were employed with gunboats of the Royal Naval Rhine Squadron as, ironically, lifeguards to cover a Rhine-crossing practice by the 2nd Division on Exercise 'Spearhead One'. Captain Henry Montgomerie-Charrington and two other officers were commended by the General Officer Commanding for their efforts to save three soldiers from drowning.

On the operational, rather than training, side the Regiment was constantly patrolling the border between East and West Germany. The Russians had given up their attempts to starve out the British, French and American garrisons in Berlin by cutting the road links to the City after the success of the Berlin Airlift in 1949. Their tactics were now to try to encroach at any place on the border which might be in dispute. Indeed at one point Major John Greenish had to take several troops from A Squadron to a spot near Reinsdorf on the border in support of the West German border guards.

Soon after the Regiment's return to Germany the King's Funeral awards were announced. Colonel Jackie Ward and Major Tony Meredith-Hardy received the MVO, forerunner of the LVO, while Regimental Corporal Major Hyland, Squadron Corporal Major Brown and Trumpet Lance Corporal Smith received various orders of the Royal Victoria Medal. These were awarded for the roles that they had taken on the Sovereign's Escort at Windsor. Similar awards went to The Blues, who had provided the Escort in London, Colonel Abel Smith and Major the Marquess Douro being their officer recipients.

An arrival in the Regiment at this time was one 2nd Lieutenant Ronald Ferguson, son, grandson and great-grandson of former Commanding Officers of the Regiment and nephew of Colonel 'Boy' Wignall. He was put in command of one of the assault troops, and, come the summer, was playing cricket for both the Regiment and, on occasions, for the division. (On one occasion he had to face the bowling of one Aircraftsman Truman, better known later as the Yorkshire and England fast bowler, Fred Truman.)

If Major Peter Herbert MC had been the instigator of getting riding going again in the Regiment after the Second World War, the results now showed; Lieutenants Victor Hoare and Hon. Nickie Beaumont brought three horses out from England to start the regimental racing stable and were soon experiencing fluctuating fortunes at racetracks at Hanover, Bad Hartzburg and Dortmund;

Captains Montgomerie-Charrington, and the Marquess of Blandford, Lieutenants Christo Phillipson and Simon Galway and the newly-arrived Ferguson were showjumping; and the Regiment seemed to acquire some twenty horses in addition to those privately owned. These were financed in part by a profitable regimental pig farm, the pigs being fed on swill from the cookhouse.

'Sunny' Blandford was also Master, and Galway 1st Whip, of the Regiment's pack of hounds which had been taken over from Major Max Gordon and Captain Hon. Julian Berry of The Blues as they left Wolfenbüttel for Windsor. The pack became the subject of some contention with the Germans in Wolfenbüttel, who objected increasingly and stridently about the conquerors riding rough-shod over the countryside in pursuit of the uneatable. Finally, quoting some edict of Hermann Goering (himself a shooting man) from pre-war days, the German authorities succeeded in having all foxhunting banned.

This understandably did not go down well with the officers. On Guy Fawkes night they gave expression to their rage in an attack, headed by the hunt hierarchy, on the house of an anti-foxhunting former German cavalry officer. A thunderflash through his letterbox not only demolished most of his hall, but also caused quite an amount of fuss. The hunt, so to speak, went out with a bang!

Perhaps due to their life-saving role on the Rhine earlier in the year, the Regiment suddenly became very good at swimming. They won the brigade, division and BAOR championships, however came to grief in the Army championships at Aldershot 'owing to an unfortunate (and unspecified) disqualification in one event'. They ended up in fourth place.

The autumn was a time for visits. The Gold Stick, Major General the Earl of Athlone, and Princess Alice stayed for a week with the Regiment in October; the Silver Stick came in November prior to the annual inspection by the Major General Commanding the Household Brigade, Major General Julian Gascoigne. On this last occasion there was some six inches of snow lying, however the band (of the 11th Hussars, The Life Guards' own being based in London) played on and the parade went ahead.

The winter was a time for change: Major Greenish left A Squadron to take over from Major Gerard Leigh as Second in Command of the Inns of Court, the latter returning to the Regiment to take command from Colonel Jackie Ward in the new year. Colonel Ward left for London to take up the appointment of Silver Stick, taking Orderly Room Corporal Major Dennis Meakin with him. Lieutenants Garry

Patterson and Viscount Weymouth left, as did Major Derek Cooper, but not before captaining the regimental skiing team. This contained Montgomerie-Charrington, Bartlett, the newly joined Lord Brooke, and Ferguson. Major Cooper freely admits that he was only captain by virtue of being the senior officer present. The team competed in the army championships in Austria, then under quadripartite occupation, similar to Germany.

Captain Kenneth Diacre rejoined after a brief career in the City and in the new year Captain the Marquess of Blandford retired, as did Regimental Corporal Major 'Alfie' Hyland, having held the appointment for nearly eight years. And Major Tony Meredith-Hardy returned from Knightsbridge to become Second in Command.

1953 was Coronation year, and also the year for the Presentation of new Standards by The Queen to the Household Cavalry. (Standards were traditionally presented every ten years but, owing to the War, this had not taken place since 1933.)

Accordingly in March 200 men and twelve officers under the command of Major Robin Wordsworth moved to Aldershot. They were there fitted for No. 1 Dress (ceremonial), a new order of dress for Household Cavalry, in time for the Standards Parade on 28 April in the Home Park beneath Windsor Castle. There the Regiment was joined by the Mounted Squadron, by an armoured car troop from the Inns of Court and by Life Guards from 67th Training Regiment RAC, the parade all being under the overall command of Lieutenant Colonel Gerard Leigh.

For the Coronation itself on 2 June, the Household Cavalry dismounted party was commanded by Major Muir Turnbull and was joined by Major Norman Hearson and twenty soldiers from the recently formed Household Cavalry Training Cadre at Windsor. The Commanding Officer himself rode as Second in Command on the Sovereign's Escort with Lieutenant Colonel David Smiley of The Blues on the other wheel of the Queen's carriage.

The Regiment were all billetted for the occasion, together with 8,500 other troops, in Earls Court. The sense of honour in taking part in the thirteen-mile march and the enthusiasm were not dampened by the pouring rain, according to the optimistic scribe for the Guards Magazine. Anyway, once their damp uniforms had been handed in, the entire party went on three weeks' leave.

Back in Wolfenbüttel the rear party was commanded by Major Meredith-Hardy with Captain Michael Wyndham, recently returned from a staff appointment in Washington, as his Adjutant. With only one composite sabre squadron left behind, they nevertheless had to keep up the schedule of border patrols and trade training during the three-month absence of the main party.

Coronation Day was a holiday. Captain Chiesman and Regimental Corporal Major Jenkins made the barracks very gay, the record states, with flags, flowers and bunting; loudspeakers were erected around the barracks so that the British Forces Network account of proceedings could be broadcast; refreshment tents were erected and a miniature sports meeting was held during the afternoon.

The Officers' House hired a (German) television set and invited prominent local Germans to watch. Among those attending was the former officer whose house had been attacked by the Hunt. The day ended with an all ranks' dance in the gymnasium.

The main party under the Commanding Officer returned at the end of June and the Regiment immediately embarked on intensive training, having been spared exercises thus far in the year. Then in September, 1953, Major General H.E. 'Pete' Pyman, the Divisional Commander and an officer of the no-nonsense Royal Tank Regiment, set them a test exercise based on his own wartime experiences in North-West Europe. For five days they were to perform many of the various tactics common to armoured reconnaissance. What Pyman had been expecting of The Life Guards is not known: however he applied afterwards for his son, Tony, to join the Regiment for his National Service, which was regarded as praise indeed.

Two weeks later the Regiment led the advance of 'Southland' against 'Northland' with such *élan* on the Rhine Army exercise 'Grand Repulse' that proceedings ended a day earlier than planned.

Autumn was the time for visiting VIPs again combined with preparing to hand over the barracks and contents to the incoming 13th/18th Hussars. General Sir Richard Gale, Commander in Chief, Northern Army Group (a part of the NATO land forces) came to say farewell, as did Lieutenant Colonel Jackie D'Avigdor Goldsmid, the General Staff Officer, Grade one (GSO1) at 11th Armoured Division on behalf of the commander, and Brigadier Q. Peddie, commander of the 91st Lorried Infantry Brigade.

The Life Guards then entrained for England, their ultimate destination being, for a change, Egypt.

Chapter 5

Return to Egypt (1954-1956)

ON ARRIVAL at Harwich Trooper Ian Swain remembers that the men were given a disgusting meal in the transit camp, a heavy mauling by Customs and promptly put on a train for Brentwood. There, rather than being met by a fleet of lorries, to their dismay they found the band waiting at the station. They marched up a hill to Warley Barracks where the Gold Stick, the Earl of Athlone, was waiting to take the salute.

Returning in the New Year from leave, the Regiment went by train to Southampton where they boarded the troopship, the *Empire Ken*, a former German steamship built in Hamburg in the 'twenties. Lieutenant Colonel Albert Lemoine, the Director of Music, and the band were there to see them off, as was the Blues' Commanding Officer, Lieutenant Colonel David Smiley OBE, MC.

Accommodation for the men was in three-tier bunks on three decks, all of which became very unpleasant in the Force Eight storm that the ship encountered on sailing. This lasted for two days, but, once the Mediterranean was reached, matters improved. They improved further still when the *Empire Ken* put into Algiers and all ranks were allowed ashore for what was, for most of them, their first taste of North Africa. 'We were amazed,' wrote Swain, 'that all the young boys had beautiful sisters to whom they were prepared to introduce us!'

A carrier from the US 6th Fleet was also in port and several officers remember seeing a group of their sailors, tall even by Life Guard standards, in their white uniforms standing in line outside establishments such as the Black Cat, which seemed very popular.

The food on board was good, with fresh bread being baked daily in the ship's bakery. There was also a cinema with a selection of the latest films (Swain remembers Genevieve) and Major David Hodson was in charge of sports training. Highlight of the boxing was the match between Lieutenant Ronald Ferguson and Trooper Preedy. The latter won on points by a 'narrow margin'.

The band of the Irish Guards, the Regiment's new neighbours in Fanara, were on the quayside to greet the ship when she docked at Port Said. The Life Guards disembarked and were soon being driven south in RASC (later to become RCT) three-tonners back to their old camp at Fanara, which was to the south of the Great Bitter Lake. The Royals had been the previous occupants, so the first priority was to paint out their eagle badges which adorned the vehicles.

It is perhaps hard to explain today why so many British soldiers were stationed along the west bank of the strip of water that, to all intents and purposes, separated Africa from Asia; more especially as they most clearly were not welcome by the native inhabitants. However the Suez Canal was still a vital link between Britain and her diminishing Empire and needed guarding, especially in view of the continuing instability of the Egyptian government. King Farouk had been deposed and had sailed into exile on his yacht, while his successor, General Neguib was in turn displaced by Colonel Gamal Abdul Nasser shortly after the Regiment had arrived.

That then was the reason why The Life Guards were there and in the process of moving into tents that had been standing for so long that they were bleached white by long exposure to the sun and sand. This was also why there were no visits outside the garrison area, and the men could only leave the camp in pairs at least; and why all vehicles had to carry an armed man in the back.

Except for the Commanding Officer, the Regimental Corporal Major and the Quartermaster, who were allowed Nissen-hut married quarters, it was an unaccompanied posting, the wives having been left behind in quarters in the area controlled by London District. There were, however, the occasional unattached young ladies around, and one in particular, nicknamed 'Tasty', was the object of hot pursuit.

Lieutenant Colonel W.H. Gerard Leigh (universally known as 'G'), in command, was a professional soldier in so far as he had made it his business to be fully qualified for the appointment. He had also past experience, both during the War and after it, of how unpleasant and boring the Canal Zone to which they were confined could be for both officers and men, so was determined to do his best to avoid this.

As a pre-war regimental polo player, he arranged to take over the well-established and much envied string of fifteen polo ponies from the Royals in the teeth of opposition from the embryo 1st Guards Brigade Saddle Club. Polo was played three times a week at Fayid in the cooler weather, and on very rare occasions at the Gezira Club in Cairo, and he soon had gathered together half a dozen officers. These included Ferguson, who was new to the game, and Toby Balding, son of Gerald Balding, the pre-war international polo player.

His Adjutant, Captain Michael Wyndham, had purchased a yacht, *Siesta*, on which to live in preference to life under canvas. (Shades of Lord Cardigan in the Crimea.) The ninety-three-ton auxiliary ketch was berthed in Famagusta, Cyprus, and had belonged to friends of Philipson's parents. Since the departing GOC British Troops, Egypt, General 'Frankie' Festing was himself a member of the Royal Yacht Squadron in Cowes and had also received outstanding reports on the Regiment from Germany, there was no trouble in obtaining the necessary permission to bring the yacht down the Canal to the Great Bitter Lake. 'Nothing like frightening your officers every day, if you can!' said Festing in approval.

Wyndham, his soldier servant and a Cypriot bosun all lived on board the yacht, in which shares were later taken by the Commanding Officer and his Second in Command. Captain Ian Baillie, or failing him Mechanical Quartermaster Corporal Arthur Thompson, looked after the engines, and generous entertainment was provided by the skipper which eased the rigours of the Canal Zone.

Another helpful visiting General was Jerry Fielden, a former Coldstreamer and Chairman of the NAAFI. Since every single item, military stores apart, that was purchased by British troops and their dependents came only through that institute, he was perhaps not altogether too surprised when G told him that the Regiment wanted to buy a water-skiing boat. The item arrived six weeks later. 'The fastest delivery that the NAAFI ever made to us,' recalls G. 'Writing paper normally took six months.'

As ever there were athletics, cricket, football and basket-ball on offer to the soldiers. For those not involved in sport, most afternoons seem to have been spent swimming in the Great Bitter Lake, some five miles distant. 'Tropical Hours' was the order of the day which meant that, after an early start to the day, no work, apart from those on patrol or other essential duty, took place after lunch.

'Essential Duty' was patrolling the (unmarked) perimeter of the Canal Zone in an effort to stop the natives stealing too much army equipment (A Squadron prevented the theft of a large number of lavatory seats) and patrolling the Canal itself to stop those same natives from stealing the copper telephone lines (again). From time to time the Regiment had to find the guard for the Commander in Chief's residence, quite a popular task which needed around sixty men.

An unusual task on one occasion during the first year of the tour was for four officers and a dozen men to ferry out new vehicles to Habbaniya near Baghdad in Iraq and to return with old ones. (Iraq in those days was within the British sphere of influence: indeed the Baghdad Pact of the following year [1955] confirmed the British right to maintain a military presence in the country.)

The trip, through Sinai, Jordan and a large tract of Iraq was most interesting as it was much the same route as that taken by the 1st Regiment in 1941. It was also the last time that Life Guards entered Iraq until A Squadron crossed the Saudi-Iraq border on active service in 1991.

Early into the tour Major Henry Montgomerie-Charrington, commanding A Squadron, had his elbow badly injured in an accident with an Egyptian lorry and had to be evacuated to England. His place was taken by one of the less conventional officers of the period, Major Kenneth Diacre, an enigma.

Diacre was adored by his men, questioned at times by his contemporaries, who found him nevertheless a good companion and, to an extent, distrusted by his superiors. However, both friend and foe gave him credit for being a good leader of men. Captain Paddy Drummond thought he remembered him as going by the surname of Deacon at Rugby; it seems now generally accepted that he was of aristocratic birth and, when he died in 1988 aged 65, it was as Count Kenneth Diacre de Liancourt.

He had joined the 1st Regiment in 1942 and had left in 1946. There followed a brief and unsuccessful career in the City. On joining again in 1952 it was apparently on the condition that he could never expect to command, a condition not fully understood by the ebullient Diacre.

That said, Diacre's first task was to provide an escort for the Commander in Chief (Lieutenant General Dick Hull) and his wife who wished to visit the Monastery of Saint Catherine on Mount Sinai. The trip was a success, so Diacre decided to return there with A Squadron, a somewhat more formidable undertaking. There were bets taken in the Officers' Mess as to whether he would succeed or not.

The squadron crossed the Bitter Lake on a tank landing craft and spent the next two days battling through the rocky terrain. 7 troop had to turn back when they entered the Wadi Feran as the route was too rough for the ponderous AEC armoured cars, and one vehicle ran out of road, injuring a crew member. Luckily there was an American drilling site nearby with a medical team who arranged for the luckless soldier to be evacuated to the British Military Hospital at Fayid.

The Greek Orthodox Monastery itself is of great fame and antiquity. The squadron were conducted around it. Former Corporal Ian Swain writes that the charnel house was a bit daunting, but that the site was most interesting as it was where Moses saw the Burning Bush and received the Ten Commandments from God. (The local joke at the time went on the following lines: Moses, addressing the Children of

Israel, 'I have good news and bad news. Firstly, there are only ten commandments; secondly, adultery is still in.')

Eric Sant was the newly promoted Squadron Corporal Major of A Squadron, Eric Lloyd receiving similar promotion in D Squadron at the same time. Swain, who went on to become a chemist with ICI, remembers being served tea laced with rum (Gunfire) in bed on Christmas morning by the former. Then at lunch he was served by the officers. These customs were traditional in the Regiment when abroad over Christmas.

The Warrant Officers and Non-Commissioned Officers' Mess, the 'heart of the Regiment', has always tended to be more active socially than the officer equivalent. A 'house warming' party was held soon after the Regiment arrived at which the Master Cook, Staff Corporal 'Charlie' Beales, excelled himself over the food.

Beales, a veteran of the Great Tram Ride in Brunswick only two years previously, was to hold the appointment of Master Cook, alternating at times with Corporal Major Troth between the Regiment and Knightsbridge, for the next fifteen years. He left as a WO2 in 1969 after twenty-five years of service with the Regiment. He also became part of Regimental lore by being the only Life Guard to swim the twenty miles across the Great Bitter Lake, less than sober and without back-up.

Meanwhile, at Regimental Headquarters Colonel G had other more weighty matters to consider. One of the contingency plans for which the Regiment was prepared was the re-occupation of Cairo and the Nile Delta. This would have been done, had the need arisen, by an advance down the Suez-Cairo road of a considerable force with The Life Guards in the van.

Another contingency, which took G, together with General Festing, up to the northern Iraq-Iran border, was the ever-present threat of the Soviet Red Army sweeping down from the north across Iraq, Jordan and Israel to seize the Canal. The General Staff in Cairo apparently envisaged the Regiment, a battalion of Highland Light Infantry and supporting arms holding back the hordes for at least a month to give them time to reinforce the Canal!

At the end of the first year the Internal Security threat diminished considerably. This was probably not unconnected with an agreement with the Egyptians that they would be allowed henceforth to run the Canal themselves on behalf of the Anglo-French owners, and that the British would start to withdraw the garrison.

Colonel G was thus able, for the first time during the tour, to exercise the full Regiment. Exercise 'Figpicker II' took place over the same terrain as had Operation 'Figpicker' in 1942 in which the 1st Regiment had taken part.

1955 also saw the arrival of, among others, 2nd Lieutenants James Rowntree, Tony Pyman and Andrew Hartigan, though Rowntree was posted to Carlisle soon after arrival.

The regimental polo team were beaten in extra time by the 3rd Royal Horse Artillery in the final of the Canal Zone Inter-Regimental tournament (seven teams had entered). The basketball team, captained by the redoubtable Corporal of Horse Singleton and coached by Company Sergeant Major Instructor Harrington, had better luck. They beat 2059 (Seychelle) Company, Royal Pioneer Corps, to win the Canal Zone basketball final, Corporal of Horse Singleton receiving the Cup from the GOC, Lieutenant General Dick Hull.

Trouble in the meantime was brewing up-country in the Aden Protectorate. At short notice and with minimal briefing a party of twenty-nine all ranks from A Squadron, a land-rover and eight of the newly arrived Mark I Ferret scout cars were loaded into Hastings aircraft and flown to Aden together with the 1st Seaforth Highlanders. Major Diacre was in command of the Regiment's contingent.

The security of the Protectorate at that time was the joint responsibility of the Governor and the Air Officer Commanding Aden. The control in the countryside was much as had been exercised by the Raj on the North-West Frontier of India in the past. Treaties would be struck with local rulers, which normally meant giving them money in return for guarantees of good behaviour.

The RAF Regiment, normally only used for static defence around RAF installations, were the only British ground troops. They also provided officers for the locally enlisted Levies. Finally there were the Government Guards, only quasi-military, but with British officers. These two groups occupied numerous primitive hill-forts in the mountains.

A 'sub-tribe' called the Shamsi had decided to move the goal-posts, had ambushed and killed two RAF officers (one a wing commander) and had laid siege to one of the forts called Robat. The fort was running very low on water and it was July.

Diacre's officers, originally 2nd Lieutenants Michael Young and Tony Pyman, acquired further reinforcements in the shape of Lieutenant John Corrie and Surgeon Captain (he was to become, by time, Surgeon Major during the following month) Geoffrey Bulow.

Bulow was delighted for any excuse to get away from the Canal Zone, where the care of 400 fit young Life Guards hardly over-extended him. As Medical Officer to the Regiment, he was fully badged as a Life Guard which confused the Seaforth Highlanders. They could not make out whether he was a complete charlatan or, as Diacre put out, his personal physician. He proved a great help to Diacre in a variety of non-medical roles.

Diacre's force set off on a four-day 360-mile journey over dreadful country and eventually met up with the Seaforths, under whose command they were, at a place called Ataq. With additional assistance from a squadron of Royal Engineers and three companies of Levies, together with air support, the attack went in. The indigo-daubed Shamsi melted away into the hill, sniping occasionally, and the fort was relieved of its siege.

Two other characters emerge from the account. The first was Donald Wise, a former captain in the Parachute Regiment who was at that time based in Nairobi as the *Daily Express* Africa correspondent. He suddenly appeared out of the blue and attached himself to Diacre's column. He particularly remembers Diacre, whom he liked, having his Teddy Bear in his land-rover. Named Aloysius (shades of *Brideshead Revisited*), the bear would receive a clip from Diacre's driver from time to time.

The other was Captain Tom Coombs of The Blues, serving three years with the Government Guards for allegedly using bad language when driving the regimental coach in London. He was nominally in charge of Fort Robat, which led Tony Pyman, in later years and after an argument between the two, to remark that he would not have tried so hard had he known that Coombs was under siege!

As Diacre's force made its way back to Egypt, Major Hodson was on his way out to Aden with his squadron to teach the RAF Regiment how to drive the Ferret scout cars. Diacre later received a confidential letter from the Silver Stick Adjutant, Major Hon. Julian Berry of The Blues, stating that the War Office wanted 'a report on how the RAF Regiment worked (or did not) and any other bad points that you noticed that could be used against them'.

Diacre's lengthy report concluded: 'They are thoroughly moderate soldiers with little training either disciplinary or tactical, with bad NCOs and mediocre officers — the latter ill equipped in military training or knowledge.' Berry passed the War Office's thanks to Diacre and it was perhaps no coincidence that, when the Regiment moved to Aden three years later, the RAF Regiment were confined to guarding airfields.

In the autumn Field Marshal Sir John Harding was appointed Military Governor of Cyprus, where trouble was starting to flare up with some of the inhabitants who wanted union with Greece (Enosis). He asked for a Life Guard escort which was promptly assembled and sent in October to the island under the command of Lieutenant David Cape.

Meanwhile the Canal Zone was starting to resemble a ghost town. Such installations that the Egyptians were not prepared to buy were left to the sand, which soon overwhelmed them. The loss of the Palladium open-air cinema just outside the barrack gate was a blow to the soldiers; the last polo tournament was held, as was the last swimming gala. The period was enlivened by the arrival of 2nd Lieutenant John Fuller, son of Major Sir Gerard Fuller Bt who had commanded a squadron in the 1st Regiment during the war. The period was also saddened by the pending resignation of the Adjutant, Captain Wyndham.

Michael Wyndham came from a long line of Life Guard Wyndhams, indeed he was the son of Colonel Humphrey Wyndham MC, a former Commanding Officer. He was due, however, to be cited as a co-respondent in a forthcoming divorce case. The received wisdom at the time was that those involved in any way in a divorce should not be allowed anywhere near the Royal Family. No divorced person could, for instance, enter the Royal Enclosure at Royal Ascot nor, following the same argument, be a member of Household Troops.

G was reluctant to lose Wyndham, who had proved to be a good Adjutant and a popular officer. In order to cover his own position, however, he had to ask Wyndham for a letter of resignation. This he proposed to keep in his desk and only make use of should Wyndham's involvement in the divorce become public knowledge. It eventually did, and after a period as an instructor at Sandhurst which preceded the court case, he went.

The only humour in the otherwise sad tale was provided by the Royal Navy. The Londoner's Diary from the *Evening Standard*, picking up the story of Wyndham's resignation and the reasons behind it, telephoned the Admiralty to ask what the Naval guide-line would be in those circumstances. 'In view of the example set by the late Lord Nelson,' replied a laconic spokesman, 'their lordships take a rather more liberal view of these matters!'

Then, at Christmas, there came an urgent call for a squadron to go to Cyprus *instanter*. A Squadron were detailed, Diacre again, and sailed at full strength on a Landing Ship, Tank (LST) before the turn of the year. All of the new Ferrets went with them, in addition another newcomer, a Saracen six-wheeled armoured personnel carrier, as an experimental command vehicle. The tour was marred by the death of Corporal of Horse Mick Brown, killed when his armoured car overturned after the verge gave way on the Nicosia road. He was a fine example of a Life Guard whom Diacre had particularly asked should come with the squadron. Corporal Brian Harwood, his gunner-operator at the time, remembers how keenly his death was felt in the squadron. Brown was buried in Nicosia.

The remainder of the Regiment moved to Moascar in January, 1956, where they were joined briefly by the advance party of The Blues en route for Cyprus. They collected HQ and C Squadrons' vehicles to take with them, and departed. Those two squadrons sailed for home in March, while D Squadron remained for a further month and, together with the 2nd Grenadiers with whom they stayed, were the last troops out of Egypt *only for a matter of months*. For on 26 July President Nasser announced that he was nationalizing all foreign interests, including the Suez Canal.

The Suez Crisis has been covered extensively over the years and it is not the purpose here to go into the political arguments that still rage today. Suffice it to say that neither Great Britain nor France were prepared to sit idly by and watch a third world country seize their assets, both financial and strategic. Eventually joint military action was taken, with Israel enthusiastically joining in. However strong pressure from the Americans, regardless of their own occupation of the Panama Canal Zone, halted the invasion before it had achieved its objectives.

Nor is this an account of gallant action by the Regiment: only one vehicle, the officers' mess truck, was actually landed in Egypt (and very difficult it proved to get back) and the majority of Life Guards never left territorial waters.

The Regiment had returned to Windsor in the Spring in dribs and drabs to find Combermere Barracks, which they had left in the full glory of its Victorian squalor four years before, under renovation. Although this was to continue over the next dozen years, the four new barrack blocks, each with central heating, hot and cold running water and inside lavatories were certainly an improvement.

Colonel G, having served his allotted span, moved to London to become Silver Stick, and also to be largely instrumental in launching the Household Brigade Polo Club on Smith's Lawn in Windsor Great Park. His place was taken by Lieutenant Colonel Tony Meredith-Hardy MVO, with Major John Greenish as Second in Command. Lieutenant Garry Patterson rejoined the regiment and 2nd Lieutenants Jake Rothschild and Simon Cooper were among the National Service officers to arrive. Viscount Galway became Adjutant.

Simon Galway, the 9th Viscount of an Irish creation, was probably the last of the 'Corinthians' to serve in The Life Guards. Hard-riding, hard-drinking and autocratic, he was nonetheless a determined man with a kindly side to his nature. He left the Regiment in 1960 only to die eleven years later at the age of forty-one, having truly burnt the candle at both ends.

It was also Galway who lost the Top Secret plans, only to be opened after sailing, of the invasion of Egypt in a scene reminiscent of the luckless RAF officer's loss of the secret lap-top computer during the 1991 Gulf War. Although rumour had it that he left the plans in a taxi outside White's, they were in fact taken, together with his car and his guns, from outside his London flat. (The helpful Metropolitan Police found the car, together with the unopened plans, within hours, returning them to Galway without asking embarrassing questions.)

After Nasser's July declaration, the military machine started to move: a block was put on all demobilization — Major Henry Montgomerie-Charrington was due out on that same day — the Z category reservists were recalled; and the Regiment was sent down to Rollestone Camp on Salisbury Plain. They were also issued with a Padre.

Padres are rarely seen in England, being centralized at places such as Bagshot Park, their Headquarters. Abroad they are normally to be found at garrison level but, given a hint of active service, they are issued on a scale of one per regiment or battalion. The Regiment was issued with an Irish Rugby International who later was to win the Military Cross during the final withdrawal from Aden. Captain the Reverend Robin Roe, who once threw Galway into the fireplace for swearing in his presence, was a great man in more senses than one. Not only had he twenty caps to his credit, but also a collar-size of 19 ½!

A less welcomed visitor was the Divisional Commander, Major General 'Jolly Jack' Churcher. With inadequate briefing that typified visits to the Regiment by senior officers (Major General Anthony Farrar-Hockley did likewise before the Regiment returned to Ulster in 1972) he addressed the senior ranks, after being introduced by Lieutenant General Sir Hugh Stockwell. 'I don't know if you lot know much about the Suez Canal,' started the General. Mutterings were heard from the men, who had been the last British troops to leave the Canal only months before.

The vehicles were eventually loaded on to three ships at Southampton and sailed away with Major Hodson and a small party to escort them. The main party, with a lot of bored reservists, sat in

Rollestone with no equipment, nor vehicles. Major Toni Chiesman organized a treasure-hunt for those officers who had private cars, which involved visiting most of the public houses on Salisbury Plain.

Major Muir Turnbull on the other hand recalls that the Regiment were ordered to send armoured car crews to a variety of different depots around the country to draw up yet more vehicles which were to rendezvous at Newport as part of the Master Plan, code-named Operation 'Magic'. With no form of communications, nor office, at his disposal he commandeered an AA telephone box from which he and Lieutenant Michael Young managed to gather all the vehicles in.

Captain Wyndham was recalled from Sandhurst, where he was an Instructor while awaiting his retirement, and told to take a squadron convoy to Barry Docks in Wales, and on a Bank Holiday. After he reached Gloucester he decided to take a detour through the Forest of Dean in an effort to avoid the worst of the holiday traffic.

A squadron on the move takes up over a mile in length, and the speed is set by that of the slowest vehicle, invariably the Scammell recovery vehicle. After a time the squadron had attracted a twelve-mile tail-back on the twisty route. Wyndham, in the lead vehicle, remembers an irate civilian motorist berating him as he eventually managed to pass the column. 'Don't blame me, mate,' shouted Wyndham in reply. 'Blame Colonel Nasser!'

'I don't give a bugger what the name of your Commanding Officer is,' was the reply from the ill-informed driver.

Trooper Peter Ashman had recently joined up as a regular soldier after an apprenticeship in the printing trade. (He was later to become A Squadron Clerk.) While recalling that army life was not unlike his childhood in a National Children's Home, he admits to having been a little apprehensive about going to war after a rather compressed basic training.

The Regiment was eventually embarked on the troopship *Empire Orwell*. Conditions were fairly cramped and the ship, while in dock, was 'dry'. Officers were reduced to throwing rolled-up five-pound notes to passing dockers on the quay and asking them to buy them whisky from off-licences.

2nd Lieutenant Andrew Wills climbed to the top of one of the giant quayside cranes for a bet, and Captain William Edgedale took a sea-sick pill. A bad sailor and detecting movement of the ship during the night, he swallowed a 'Kwell' and went to sleep. The following morning he extolled the virtues of the product at length before going on deck. The ship had indeed shifted — 300 yards to the next quay having been moved by tugs.

12. Capt Michael Wyndham's yacht *Siesta* on the Great Bitter Lake, Egypt, in 1955.

13. Tpr Brian Harwood and Cpl Derek Stratford with their Daimler armoured car in the Suez Canal Zone, Egypt, 1955. (*Brian Harwood*)

14. Gold Stick and Silver Stick: Maj-Gen the Earl of Athlone and Col
Jackie Ward in Wellington Barracks, 1955.*(War Office)*

15. Cpl Ian Swain with skull, St. Catherine's Monastery, Sinai, in 1955. (*Ian Swain*)

16. 'A fine example of a Life Guard': CoH Mick Brown, killed in an accident in Cyprus, 1956. (*from a painting in the WO's and CsoH Mess*)

17. FM Sir John Harding, Governor of Cyprus, with A Squadron. SCM Eric Sant behind. In foreground Mk1 Ferret, background White half-track APC. (*Household Cavalry Museum*)

18. Recruits for Knightsbridge in 1955: Instructor (centre) CoH Peter
Lewery and Cpl Brian Harwood (rt). Note the white lanyards on the
left shoulders of the RHG troopers. (*David Barry*)

19. Dingo scout-car, 1957, commanded by LCpl Tonkins. (*Household
Cavalry Museum*)

20. A Squadron (Maj Toni Chiesman, SCM Eric Sant) in 1957 in front of the old Officers' House, Combermere Barracks, Windsor. The site is where the Cookhouse now stands. (*David Barry*)

21. A Sovereign's Escort forms up in The Life Guards' end of the yard in the old Knightsbridge Barracks in the 'fifties. (*A Rowlinson*)

22. The Life Guard Mounted Squadron, 1958: from the right Maj Toni Chiesman, Tptr Cpl Tither, CoH Tom Gardner, SCM John Cawthorne, Capt William Edgedale. (*David Barry*)

23. Route lining for the Garter Ceremony, Windsor Castle, 1959. (*Keystone Press*)

24. The last of the 'Dutch' horses: Siegfried in the Officers' dining-room in Knightsbridge, 1959, with Maj Toni Chiesman. On the wall is the painting of the Drum-horse by Sir Alfred Munnings. (*Keystone Press*)

25. Silver Stick: Col Gerard Leigh in 1959. Note the wand of office beside the helmet. *(Hay Wrightson)*

26. Saladin up-country at Fort Ataq, Aden Protectorate, 1959. *(M Austin)*

After three days of inactivity, during which time a cease-fire had been called by the Americans, everyone was allowed off the ship and went back to Combermere. Hodson meanwhile was 'somewhere in the Mediterranean' sending the occasional signal back to England to try and find out what was going on.

Eventually his particular ship docked in Cyprus, where Lieutenant Colonel the Marquess Douro was stationed in command of The Blues. They were incredibly helpful and between them they managed to prevent 'various gentleman of foreign nationalities masquerading as military with arm-bands marked UNO' from off-loading all the vehicles, bar the Officers' Mess truck, at Port Said. It finally took the intervention of Field Marshal Sir John Harding from Cyprus to recover the latter.

The ships eventually returned to England and, with unusual co-operation from the dockers, were back at Combermere in time for Christmas. It was, however, found that a great many tools were missing from the armoured car tool kits, including such valueless, but essential, items such as sun-compasses, and many personal belongings.

So ended the Suez Crisis for The Life Guards. The lessons that were learned, in so far as they affected the Regiment, were speed of reaction and air portability. It signalled the death-knell for the troopship and the advent of the age when all men and equipment, bar tanks and heavy engineer plant, would in the future increasingly be moved by air.

Once the Regiment were all back together, the establishment was changed from what, in effect, was a War Establishment: all of the 7 Troops, with their cumbersome AEC armoured cars, were out and C Squadron was reorganized as the Air Portable, or AP, Squadron. This consisted of five Sabre troops, each of four of the new Ferret Mark II scout cars which were mounted with the American .30 Browning medium machine-gun. Squadron Headquarters and the Echelon were carried in Land-rovers.

Chapter 6

Aden and Oman (1958-1959)

1957 STARTED on a sad note with the death of Major General the Earl of Athlone, Gold Stick and Colonel of the Regiment, who had held the appointment since 1936. Although in line regiments it is the practice to offer the colonelcy to retired senior officers of the particular regiment in question for a five-year, exceptionally a ten-year, period, in the Household Brigade it has been the custom (the Coldstream excepted) to nominate to the Queen a member of the Royal Family, or a distinguished military man. Athlone's predecessor, for example, had been Field Marshal the Viscount Allenby, of Palestine fame in the First World War.

Athlone had been both and his successor was a Field Marshal: Sir John Harding was shortly to finish his term as Military Governor of Cyprus where, of course, he had encountered A Squadron two years previously. Although deficient in all but two of his fingers on his left hand, he nevertheless managed without difficulty to hold four reins and the Gold Stick itself (a wand of office) when on parade.

He was only to hold office for a mere seven years before retiring for personal reasons, but during that period he really endeared himself to all ranks. Elevated to the peerage in 1958, 'Colonel John' was a soldier's soldier and his resignation in 1964 was received with genuine sadness.

On one occasion, when making his annual speech at the Officers' Dinner in the early 'sixties, he rather piqued Major Toni Chiesman, who by now was as fanatical about his hunting as Captain Ronald Ferguson had become over polo. 'We must not,' said Colonel John, 'allow ourselves to become a regiment of fox-hunting gunners.'

This brought predictable boos from Major (retired) the Viscount Galway, another hard man to follow across country, and Chiesman, both seated at the special table which was reserved traditionally for the more vociferous and rumbustious members.

Other more routine departures during the Spring included Rev. Robin Roe (to the Parachute Brigade) and Lieutenant Colonel (QM) E.S. Nicholls (to become Quartermaster to the RAEC Depot). Nick Nicholls had been with the Regiment for thirty years, for the latter part of his service as Quartermaster both to the Regiment and at

Knightsbridge. He was to remain in close contact with the Regiment as secretary of the Officers' Dining Club.

He was succeeded by Lieutenant (QM) Denny Roberts, who was commissioned, along with Lieutenant (QM) Dennis Meakin.

Arrivals included 2nd Lieutenants Arthur Gooch, Michael Hare (son of the then Secretary for War, later to be Lord Blakenham), Lord Valentine Thynne (following in the footsteps of his two elder brothers, all sons of the Marquess of Bath) and William Loyd; also the return from civilian life of Lieutenant Christopher Wordsworth.

The summer, the first uninterrupted one at home for six years, passed peacefully enough with a little cricket, polo, showjumping and tent-pegging for those so inclined, and the occasional exercise on Salisbury Plain, or in East Anglia with the 1st Guards Brigade. The Air Portable Squadron, as C Squadron had become, were now part of the Strategic Reserve, so were not directly under regimental control, and would come and go as their superiors dictated.

Some unwelcome, but trivial, publicity came the Regiment's way at the time. The first concerned the Adjutant, Galway. An exchange of blows between him and Captain Mike Thomas in the Orderly Room led to the former's departure to a staff appointment in the recruiting branch of the War Office at short notice. Captain Ronald Ferguson, who was at the time Second in Command to Major Toni Chiesman in A Squadron, was dragged, like Thespis from the chorus, to fill the vacancy.

The second event to make the gossip columns concerned Lieutenant David Curtis-Bennett, son of the then well-known QC. He had been dining well, if not wisely, in the Cavalry Club with the newly promoted Captain Christopher Wordsworth. On descending from the first-floor dining-room towards the marble-flagged hall, he tripped and fell over the bannisters.

Luckily he fell onto the table at the foot of the stairs, which broke his fall, and he escaped with only minor injuries. The tabloid press had a field day. Senior members of the club were quoted as comparing the noise of the crash with that of the German bomb which fell on the Cafe de Paris in the Second World War; the question also was raised over whether or not he should resign from the club.

The winter of 1957 saw the opening of the present Officers' House, — a luxury dwelling compared with its predecessor. Curiously, while digging the foundations for the building, the workmen unearthed a 2-pounder barrel. What it was doing there, and how it came to be buried in what was the barrack field, have never been resolved.

Before Christmas the Regiment was warned for a posting to

Hildesheim in Germany, news greeted with some joy by the married men. Serving in the Rhine Army was held to be a comfortable posting. The married quarters were better than many in England, the local overseas allowance (LOA) was generous and the drink and cigarettes were Duty Free.

1958 saw the arrival of two future racehorse trainers, 2nd Lieutenants Richard Head, whose former Life Guard father was a previous Minster of Defence, and Nick Gaselee. It also saw the departure of Lord Valentine Thynne, an event mourned by the other subalterns. For Thynne had been awarded so many extra duties during his brief period with the Regiment that the rest scarcely performed more than one spell as Orderly Officer per month!

Captain Ian Baillie, soon to take command of A Squadron, took up rally driving. In the days when the sport was still largely amateur he was well placed in the Monte Carlo rally until meeting a snowdrift which, unsportingly, concealed a brick wall. The sight of Baillie's short figure behind the wheel of his Jaguar soon earned him the affectionate nickname of 'Toad' after the character in *Wind in the Willows*, a name that was to remain with him for the rest of his life.

In February the Household Cavalry held a dedication service for those who had given their lives in the Second World War, at the Holy Trinity church, Windsor, where the Rev. Eric Dawson-Walker officiated. After Colonel Sir Robert (Eric) Gooch, who by now had two sons and a nephew serving with the Regiment, had read the lesson, former Regimental Corporal Major Jobson paraded the Roll of Honour down the aisle, escorted by Squadron Corporals Major Cawthorne, and Evans of The Blues.

The Roll was then handed to Colonel Andrew Ferguson and Colonel Sir Henry Abel Smith, who in turn passed it to the vicar to be laid up. After the service Colonel Ferguson commanded the marching party of both serving and retired Life Guards, including his son as Adjutant, back to barracks.

During March the Regiment received the less-than-welcome news that they were going in the autumn, not to Germany, but on an largely unaccompanied tour to the Aden Protectorate. (There were a limited amount of quarters for officers and men in the Crater district in Aden.)

They also held a spectacular Parade for Lord Harding of Petherton, their newly elevated Colonel, which incorporated both the armoured car regiment and the Mounted Squadron, on the Cavalry Review ground in Windsor Great Park. The twenty-one-gun salute that followed was short-changed by one as Lieutenant Michael Young forgot to 'set the trip' on the 2-pounder in his Daimler armoured car. On a sartorial point, the armoured car regiment all wore battle-dress, while the mounted squadron wore service-dress and carried service, rather than state, swords. The dutymen wore the old style tunics, which buttoned up to the neck, bandoliers and puttees.

At around this time a decision was taken to do away with the appointment of Technical Adjutant, a post held at the time by Captain Ned Boldero who was due to leave anyway. A new post of Technical Quartermaster (Tech QM) was created, the first incumbent being Lieutenant (Tech QM) Arthur Thomson, the last of the wartime regimental fitters.

After a summer spent in preparations for the move and pre-embarkation leave, on 19 August, 1958, the main party embarked on the *Dilwara* in Southampton. The advance party under Major David Hodson had sailed on the *Dunera* two weeks previously.

As was normal on such occasions, there seemed to be more people waving goodbye than there were soldiers to be waved at. There were the officers of the Mounted Regiment, resplendent in their breeches and boots, both Gold Sticks, Colonel Jackie D'Avigdor-Goldsmid from the AG17 branch of the War Office, Major General Rodney Moore, commanding the Household Brigade, and Major General Claude Pert from the Household Brigade Polo Club, to name but a few.

The Director of Music, Lieutenant Colonel Albert Lemoine, and the band were on the quayside, and played for two hours before the ship finally sailed. Also left behind were Regimental Corporal Major Henderson, his service over, and Majors Duncan Llewellyn and Mike Thomas who had retired.

The *Dilwara* arrived off the port of Aden on the evening of 3 September, 1958, so it was decided not to dock until the following morning. Consequently the heat in the cabins of the now motionless ship became intolerable, and the officers decided to sleep on deck.

For those who participated in team games, deck cricket had proved popular during the voyage, Captain Ferguson and Corporal of Horse Singleton again being the regimental stars. A concert on board had also been popular, the officers' act consisting, unoriginally, of a tuneless rendering of 'Lloyd George knew my Father' to the tune of 'Onward Christian Soldiers'.

The troopships plied regular scheduled runs around the globe, so the *Dilwara* was by no means solely for use by the Regiment, even if at times it seemed that way. Indeed, there had already apparently been some unpleasantness with the Captain who awoke one morning to find the regimental flag at the masthead.

The regimental flag, the regimental cypher on a red and blue halved background, features fairly regularly during this story. Infantry regiments had their Colours, the line cavalry their Guidons, but the Standards of The Life Guards remain firmly lodged with the Mounted Squadron. The Regiment attached neither significance, nor ceremonial, to their flag — it was just reassuring to see it around.

Once the Regiment had disembarked, they began the process of taking over from the 13th/18th Hussars. A Squadron were initially based with Regimental Headquarters and Headquarter Squadron at Little Aden, and one of their first tasks was to occupy outposts up country at Am Nu'am and Dhala. D Squadron, under Major Diacre, were flown up to Oman, some 1,200 miles away, to help the Sultan's Armed Forces (SAF), who had a slight problem on their hands.

The situation in the Arabian peninsula at that time was complex, to say the least. The majority of the land-mass, including the two big deserts, the Nafud and the Rub al Khali (the Empty Quarter), was Saudi Arabian territory; the southern coastal strip comprised the East and West Aden (British) Protectorates, with an increasingly unstable Kingdom of Yemen to the north; to the east was the Sultanate of Muscat and Oman, hereinafter referred to as Oman; and on the north-eastern coast of the Persian Gulf were a succession of independent sheikhdoms and 'kingdoms' stretching from the Strait of Hormuz in the east to Iraq in the west.

Her Majesty's Government had treaties of friendship with Oman and with the Gulf States. Indeed the seven who were later to form the Union of Arab Emirates (UAE) and Oman's native forces were all commanded by British officers, either seconded from regular duty, or else on contract as mercenaries. The treaties had initially been signed in the last century to control the piracy on the coast, with little attention being paid to what happened inland. But now, with the discovery of ever-increasing oil reserves in the area, and with increasing efforts by both Russia and America, for their own separate reasons, to destabilize the British influence, the pace was hotting up.

An insurrection in Oman earlier in the decade had been only partially crushed: Ghalib (the Imam of Oman), his brother Talib and Suleiman, the three ringleaders, had retired to a great mountain fortress, the Jebel Akhdar (Arabic for 'Green Mountain') in the northern half of Oman. To keep matters in perspective, the mountain was about forty miles long, twenty wide, with a 6,000-foot high limestone massif that had defied attacks by the Persians in ancient history.

Matters were further confused by the fact that HMG found itself to be supporting an absolute ruler, Sultan Said bin Taimur of Oman. He condoned slavery, forbade medical aid, education or motor-cars for his impoverished people, many of whom suffered from leprosy and glaucoma, and ruled through his Walis with the Sharia Law. The dungeons in the forts at Nizwa and Jalali were prime examples of his views on penal reform.

He also maintained a ban on proselytization (medical missionaries were sometimes allowed in, but only to practise medicine), and on the media. Diacre, however, was one jump ahead of him there, and was in constant and illegal contact with John Grant, the Defence correspondent of *The Times*.

On the positive side was that SAF was commanded by Colonel David Smiley of The Blues, on secondment, as was his DAA&QMG, Major Kenneth Timbrell of the Royals. Smiley, a legend in his lifetime after his exploits with Special Operations Executive (SOE) in the Second World War, was determined to remove the rebels from the Jebel. They were becoming increasingly bold; mines were being laid by them on the roads at the foot of the Jebel and supplies were reaching them without any trouble from the Saudis and their American friends.

He was delighted when Major Kenneth Diacre arrived to join him at his headquarters at Bait al Falaj as they had both been members of the 1st Household Cavalry Regiment. 'He was that rare kind of regular officer who combined competence with imagination, a sense of humour, and a highly individual approach to every problem,' he wrote.* 'Given a squadron with very young and inexperienced subalterns as troop leaders, he quickly transformed it, with the help of some first class NCOs, into an extremely efficient and happy fighting force.'

Diacre's advance party had consisted of Captain Tony Pyman, Lieutenant Arthur Gooch — 'I rate him the best armoured car troop leader that I have ever come across' he was later to write — and 2nd Lieutenant Nick Gaselee. They were met on arrival by Captain Michael Young who, Diacre recalled, had already 'gone native'. Young, an engaging officer, was nicknamed 'Just William' for a time owing to his likeness to Richmal Crompton's character and was renowned for 'going native'. Owing to his fondness for foreign and hot postings, he

* see *Arabian Assignment*, published in 1975

53

was later sent on secondment to the Tanganyka Rifles, however, after a time they mutinied (Young swears that it was not on his account), so he came back to regimental duty.

The squadrons both in Oman and in Little Aden were equipped with Ferret scout cars Mark II, a great improvement on the Mark I in that they had turrets in which were mounted .30 Browning machine-guns. They were disabled by the American heavy mines — Corporal of Horse Gilliland was blown up three times during that period, and Lieutenant Gooch once lost three out of his four Ferrets within a forty-eight hour period — but they gave a degree of protection to the crews. Another 'new' vehicle to the Regiment was the six-wheeled Saladin armoured car. (Although later in Germany they were integrated into the sabre troops, on this tour all eight were held in a heavy troop in the Protectorate and commanded by Corporal of Horse Derek Stratford.)

Meanwhile back in Little Aden Lieutenant Colonel Tony Meredith-Hardy was feeling besieged. Part of his command (D Squadron) was 1,200 miles away and not exactly under his control; and his relationships with Headquarters, British Forces Arabian Peninsula, in particular with the Deputy Land Commander, one Brigadier Hutton, were strained, to say the least. Although in radio contact with Diacre, he preferred the written word.

'I insist, my dear boy, that you use some of these vehicles [Ferrets] to travel in yourself,' he wrote to Diacre in October, when hearing about the mines. 'Dear Kenneth, we all miss you very much. Gertrude [Galway] and Toad [Baillie] are intolerable without your influence.'

And again, in November on hearing that 2nd Lieutenant Nick Gaselee had led a donkey patrol 'further into the Jebel than any white man had ventured for some years', 'I know that you watch the scope of these patrols very carefully as we do not want Talib to take any of our officers prisoner. I do not want to take home a lot of knackerless officers.' (This referred to the Arab custom of removing the genitalia of their captured enemies.)

He had further problems when Radio Cairo, broadcasting to the Arab world, put it out that the Sultan of Oman, a lackey of the British, had 50,000 of their soldiers in his country, and that the British flag flew above that of the Sultan! This aroused the Sultan from his lethargy in his palace at Salala on the Indian Ocean in southern Oman. He gave orders that the regimental flag, which flew at Diacre's Squadron Headquarters next to the SAF headquarters at Bait al Falaj, should come down. Smiley refused to pass the order on, even though it came via the Consul General. 'It [the flag] will not be taken down without my express orders. I am absolutely adamant on this point,' Meredith Hardy wrote to Diacre.

Smiley in the meantime had been taking some positive measures. With friends such as Julian Amery and Christopher Soames in high places, he had been allowed to count on two squadrons of the 22nd Special Air Service regiment (22 SAS) with which to assault the rebel stronghold on the Jebel. One squadron arrived out in November,1958, and on one of their first reconnaissance patrols lost an NCO to sniper fire.

Finally HMG agreed that D Squadron could be used 'in support' of the SAS, together with SAF and some troops from the Trucial Oman Scouts. Colonel Tony Deane-Drummond of the SAS arrived on New Year's Day and the attack was planned for 25 January, 1959. D Squadron's five Sabre troops were to 'hold the ring' around the base of the mountain, while the second in commmand, Captain Tony Pyman, with an ad hoc platoon were to climb it behind the SAS. Pyman remembers it well:

> Shortly after Christmas I was at Nizwa in control of half of the squadron awaiting our daily radio call, which was scheduled for an inconveniently early hour. When it came, it was in (Slidex) code which, when deciphered instructed me to climb the mountain with a machine-gun platoon in support of 22nd SAS.
>
> I didn't regard this as particularly welcome, but drew up a pair of army boots [officers normally wore soft desert boots, or shoes] and broke them in before the attempt was made during the period of the new moon at the end of January. The route that we were to take was to be a complete secret until the last moment.
>
> The formation of the platoon was by no means easy, with most of the men being committed to the sabre troops. Staff Sergeant Stickley of the Royal Signals was platoon sergeant, the section leaders being Corporals MacKnocker, McNab and Fettes and the men were mostly new arrivals from Windsor, augmented by various attached personnel.
>
> Each section was equipped with two Browning machine-guns from the Ferrets, and these were to be carried up the Jebel by donkeys which had just arrived for that purpose from the plains of Somalia!
>
> And so this machine-gun platoon assembled on 24 January in the foothills of the Jebel, under command of 22 SAS. Orders were of the briefest, presumably in deference to security, and

we were not even allowed to look at the area that we were about to ascend in case someone was watching us.

The long climb began at about 0200 hours, following a squadron of SAS. Our first disturbing discovery was that very few of the little donkeys (the native ones were far bigger) were prepared to climb, and nothing that we could do would induce them to do so. Again, this discovery would have been made earlier had the commander of the operation permitted even the briefest of recces/rehearsals. Clearly he had not heard that well known cavalry adage that 'time spent in reconnaissance is seldom wasted'.

Anyway, the fact that the donkeys would not perform meant that all the machine-guns, and their ammunition, had to be carried by the platoon, in addition to their own personal arms and equipment. I ended up with a belt of ammunition round my neck, as well as my rifle. It all made a difficult and tiring climb that much worse.

Just after first light we apparently came under fire, and at the same time the grenades in the pack of an SAS trooper exploded, killing him and badly injuring two of his companions. A casevac helicopter was on the scene with commendable speed, and one of the men eventually survived. I am of the opinion that this accident was caused by an accidental discharge, a theory hotly denied by the SAS. When all is said and done, I was very close to the incident.

After passing a cave containing some dead bodies, the climb came to an end and as I stood gazing in relief across the Jebel, that unattractive pinging noise started — rebel fire. I was so tired that I hardly cared!

Our role over the next few days was to hold the left flank. I became impatient and went to see the SAS commander, who was shaving in his mess tin. He gave me the impression that he didn't care very much if we were there or not. After a few more days we were ordered to return to Nizwa, and I must say that the climb down was almost as bad as the climb up!

The whole operation was a remarkable achievement, and certainly the most arduous in which I ever personally participated.

Ghalib, Talib and Suleiman evaded the cordon and escaped to their friends in Saudi Arabia. However, SAF now built an airstrip and a base on the top of the Jebel Akhdar, which has been passive ever since. All British regular troops left Oman before 1 April, 1959 — HMG's deadline in view of a forthcoming discussion in the United Nations on Oman — Diacre's squadron flying down to Aden.

Diacre, Squadron Corporal Major Eric Lloyd and Corporal MacKnocker were all Mentioned in Despatches — ironically in that the campaign medal, a clasp to the General Service Medal entitled 'Arabian Peninsula' was only awarded two years later after intense pressure from Smiley.

For Diacre, who had been warned by Meredith-Hardy in February that he was to take C Squadron, to be formed in Windsor from the Air Portable Squadron and the recently revived B Squadron, to Germany in the Autumn, it was the end of the campaign. 'It is vital that this squadron is the best possible and well led. That is why I am sending you,' wrote Hardy to Diacre.

If D Squadron had the glory, life for A Squadron had not been one of idleness. Lieutenant Timothy Gooch, the younger of Colonel Eric's two sons, and his troop spent the best part of four months up country in Dhala, an eight-hour journey inland, together with a battalion of Aden Protectorate Levies (APL). Yemen claimed the whole of the Protectorate as its own and Dhala, being near the border, was at risk from dissidents armed and encouraged by Yemen.

The troops could use their Browning machine-guns if fired upon, but could only fire across the border if engaged by more than rifle fire.

Gooch went down with malaria shortly after arrival which necessitated Lieutenant John Fuller coming up to take temporary command of his troop. Once recovered he found the delights of an independent command initially very much to his taste. His duties were mainly providing fire-power for the APL during their border patrols and village searches, and providing escorts for the fortnightly supply convoys which had to come, with another escorting troop, up the Dhala pass.

'Tomorrow another convoy... it has a Life Guard troop escorting it which will be here 'till Monday, also Christopher Wordsworth and Geoffrey Bulow are coming up.... Hurrah! To hell with the pompous APLs,' wrote Gooch to his mother in September, 1958.

The arrival of a convoy signified the arrival of sufficient drink to last, in theory, for the next fortnight. However since there was the other escorting troop and the odd 'swanners' from the Regiment to entertain, it was not unusual for the entire liquor stock to be consumed in one night.

Come mid-November, however, the novelty was wearing a bit

thin. ' I am beginning to feel that I have been long enough at Dhala,' Gooch wrote. 'If all goes according to plan I should be relieved by [Lieutenant] Simon Cooper and his troop in about three weeks.'

Meanwhile the other A Squadron troops had been deployed on a monthly rotation to An Nuam, a bleak tented camp in the desert some forty miles west of Aden. Together with a company of infantry they controlled the western approaches as far as Barim Island on the Red Sea. Lieutenant Simon Cooper (3 Troop), returning from a long patrol one evening, noticed that one of his Ferrets appeared deficient of its commander, Corporal Ken Whalley.

They found him about five miles back, embarrassed and sun-burnt. He had moved from the small turret to the engine-deck, while on the move, in an effort to keep cool, and had fallen off!

Gooch and his troop returned to Aden and to a very different world. Lieutenant Richard Head had become ADC to the Governor: HE's daughter, Diana Luce, was young, beautiful, chaste and chased by both Head and Lieutenant Nic Paravicini. Polo was being played on ponies shipped up from Kenya. And Lieutenant the Viscount Cranley was in charge of the Officers' Mess garden.

Michael Cranley had entered regimental lore earlier in the tour when two of his Ferrets became bogged down on the beach near Sohar in the face of an incoming tide. His Lordship was no more successful than Canute in his efforts to stem the waves, and as a last resort the squadron leader had to consider blowing them up with explosives if they could not be salved. Luckily, come low tide, the Land-rovers managed to pull them onto terra firma.

Cranley had had constructed a goldfish pool in the patch that passed for a garden and now required to stock it. He ordered some fish from a pet-shop in Aden, then as an afterthought asked if he could obtain some sand for the bottom of the pool. The proprietor gave the matter some thought, having several millions of acres of the commodity outside the back of his shop, and eventually agreed to supply some for a fee! Gooch also remembers that Cranley had a monkey of uncertain temper, and that someone had a gazelle which ended up as the chief delicacy at an NCOs' mess dinner.

Lieutenant John Fuller and Corporal of Horse McGahan were air-lifted, together with some of the Heavy Troop's Saladins, to Mukalla where the local tribes were misbehaving. Fuller stayed with Colonel Hugh Boustead, the Resident Advisor and veteran Arabist, and having come under fire, returned the fire with interest. He was perhaps the only officer to have fired the Saladin's main armament in anger.

Lieutenant Rhodri Davies on the other hand, on a goodwill visit to the Sharif of Beihan, kept the local ruler up for much of the night in the hope of being offered a dancing-girl, of which there was an abundance. He was out of luck.

With the return to the fold of D Squadron, it was the turn of A Squadron to head north-east, on this occasion to Sharjah, one of the seven Trucial States on the Persian Gulf. The Royal Air Force had a staging post there in what, to paraphrase, has been called the posterior of the world. The heat and humidity were intense, there was no natural water (limited drinking water was obtained from a distillation plant) and the area was featureless.

Gooch, however, went by sea on the LCT *Empire Skua*, complete with a caricature hard-drinking Scottish Chief Engineer. Disembarking a week later at Muscat before driving down to Nizwa, the Adjutant-to-be could not help noticing that Diacre's famed D Squadron, whom they were relieving, were a scruffy lot. He was also fascinated by the biblical way of life in the villages on the edge of the Empty Quarter, which was first crossed by the explorer Wilfred Thesiger in the previous decade, if not by the German writer Karl May in the last century.

A Squadron remained based at Sharjah for the remainder of the tour. Major Ian Baillie, who was joined by his cousin, Captain Peter Baillie, as Second in Command, carried out a Flag March round the Jebel Akhdar, losing two Ferrets to mines, and coming under fire, which was returned, near Nizwa. Colonel David Smiley was still the *Kaid* of SAF, and had been joined by Colonel Hugh Boustead as Minister for the Interior. (Ten years later A Squadron were back, again based at Sharjah, and carried out the same Flag March, this time without incident.)

Gooch returned soon afterwards to Aden to take over as Adjutant from Captain Ferguson, who had completed his allotted span. Captain Garry Patterson meanwhile had sailed for Kenya with Lieutenants Arthur Gooch and Michael Cranley, together with their troops, to take part in an exercise, so quiet had the situation in the Protectorate recently become.

The Commanding Officer took the opportunity to prepare the Regiment for service in Germany where the emphasis was now on nuclear warfare. Accordingly he gathered his officers round a map of Kenya, of all places, and started his lecture. It was clearly not his subject as he kept on talking about 'Russians' when what he meant was 'Roentgens', (a measure of radio-activity). His day was saved when an urgent call came over the radio from Sharjah to 'Fetch Sunray'!

This call, or the lesser 'Fetch Officer!' were fine as far as they went, but officers were not too conversant with the fine tuning of the radios. However, Corporal of Horse 'Jack' Smith was at hand to do the necessary. It then transpired that, rather than heavy casualties in an incident, Lieutenant James Rowntree had been placed in Close Arrest for throwing his plate of scrambled egg at the head of an RAF officer in a fit of petulance!

The Regiment's final departure from Aden, after handing over to the Royals, was perhaps the last time that they were to parade in Full Service Marching Order (FSMO); starched khaki drill shirts and shorts, regimental hose-tops below the knee; small pack, large pack, great-coats, steel helmets and webbing. In all it was a very impressive sight on the quay at Steamer Point.

The journey back was enlivened by the presence of Lieutenant Simon Crisp of The Blues, who had been on attachment with the Aden armoured car squadron; by shore-leave in Valetta; and by the presence on the quayside in Malta of Captain the Rev. Robin Roe. On arrival at Southampton at the end of November they were met by the usual senior officers, including Colonel the Marquess Douro, the newly appointed Silver Stick *vice* Colonel Gerard Leigh, who had retired from the Army.

Chapter 7

Herford: Corps Screen (1960-1962)

The Regiment reassembled in the New Year of 1960 in Herford, a middle-sized light-industrial town in Westphalia just to the north of the Dusseldorf-Hanover autobahn and about halfway between the two cities. Although this was by no means the Regiment's final trip to Germany, it was to be the last time that they were to be there with armoured cars, and to enjoy the freedom of movement that it entailed.

Harewood Barracks was built for Hitler's army in 1935 and was very comfortable indeed. The central heating in the blocks was fantastic; the armoured cars were kept in covered garages; the barracks boasted a large gymnasium, swimming pool and adjacent sports ground; and there were stables and a covered riding-school available for the asking in a nearby Royal Signals barracks.

From being of uncertain establishment since Suez, the Regiment was now back to the Peace Establishment of an Armoured Reconnaissance Regiment. The three sabre squadrons, A — Major the Viscount Galway, C — Major Derek Bartlet and D — Major Toni Chiesman, each had five sabre troops of two Saladins and two Ferrets, and an assault (6th) troop of three Saracen six-wheeled armoured personnel carriers (APCs).

Squadron Headquarters operated from two Saracen Armoured Command Vehicles (ACVs), with an Austin Champ (it could apparently operate under water!) for the squadron leader and a Ferret Mark I for the Squadron Corporal Major. The squadron echelon had four three-ton Bedford trucks, and a one-ton Fitted for Radio (FFR) truck for the Squadron Quartermaster Corporal, while the REME Light Aid Detachment (LAD) operated with a Scammell recovery vehicle and a White half-track.

The personal weapons for the armoured car crews were still the Stirling sub-machine gun (soldiers) and the .38 revolver (officers), however the Lee-Enfield .303 rifle had been superseded by the standard NATO 7.62mm FN rifle for the assault troops. Gone, too, for good was the faithful 19-set wireless, its place being taken by the C12 and C13 (HF) and B47 (VHF) radios.

The main armament of the Saladin was the 76mm gun which could, in theory at least, be effective against armour at up to a mile distant, and against area targets at up to three miles. The greatest joy of all, however, was the Saladin's electric kettle. All armoured cars in the past had carried petrol cooking stoves, but these could not be operated with any degree of safety on the move, nor when 'tactical'. The electric kettle could.

The purpose of the Regiment's presence in Germany was, as before, to counter any move westwards by the Soviet Union-led forces of the Warsaw Pact. The NATO forces, both ground and air, in mainland Europe were held to be heavily outnumbered. All that they could hope for was to cause sufficient delay to the enemy between their forward positions and the Rhine to allow reinforcements from England and America to arrive in the theatre, and to deploy.

The Life Guards and the Queen's Dragoon Guards (QDG) were directly under command of the 1st (and only) British Corps, itself consisting of three Divisions (1, 2 and 4). Their role, for the next three years, was to act as a screen for the Corps, in other words to be the first obstacle in the path of the Russian Bear, should he decide to advance. The two regiments were to hold the Warsaw Pact between the British front on the border and the River Weser for forty-eight hours, or to the last man, whichever came first.

This alarming prospect did not seem to cause Life Guards any loss of sleep. Most of them hoped that it would not happen, and most were sufficiently young, to use the words of a commander in the 1991 Gulf conflict, to believe themselves immortal anyway.

As Corps Troops, the Regiment had no tie with any of the brigades or divisions, even though their barracks were in the same town as those of the 4th Division's Headquarters. This was detrimental in a way as it reinforced prejudices that the Regiment were aloof, and did not deign to speak to what they regarded as lesser regiments. This was not only confined to officers: two Corporals in A Squadron had to be rebuked for failing to salute officers in the Royal Signals, their excuse being that the officers concerned were not 'proper officers'.

Friends were around, but at some distance; the QDG were at Wolfenbüttel, the 14th/20th Hussars and the Queen's Royal Irish Hussars (a recent amalgamation of Colonel 'Loopy' Kennard's 4th Hussars and the 8th Hussars) were at Hohne; other cavalry regiments were nearby at Detmold and Paderborn; and the 4th Guards Brigade, commanded at that time by Brigadier John Nelson, were to the west at Hubelrath, near Dusseldorf. Captain Christopher Wordsworth was GSOIII(Int) at the brigade's headquarters, later to be succeeded by Captain Tony Pyman.

Within the Regiment Majors Hodson and Diacre, having brought out C Squadron and the Advance Party to take over from the Royals, decided that it was time to leave, as had Major Robin Wordsworth before the Regiment left Aden. The Commanding Officer also had changed, with Lieutenant Colonel Muir Turnbull MBE taking over from the avuncular Meredith-Hardy, the latter moving to take command at Knightsbridge. Major Ian Baillie was now Second in Command, while Captain and Adjutant Timothy Gooch and Regimental Corporal Major Eric Sant remained the same.

One of the joys in store for the Regiment was a Paymaster, a commissioned officer in the Royal Army Pay Corps. The monocled Major Guy Long MC was a great character who drove around in a vintage Rolls Royce. He was put to the test early on when Major Simon Galway and Captain William Edgedale squandered the complete weekly pay for A Squadron on the gaming tables in the Travemünde Casino (the squadron were training nearby). Galway saw nothing reprehensible over his actions; he merely sent a message down to the 'Nine of Clubs', as paymasters tended to be called, and invited him to send some more money up so that he could pay his soldiers. Long obliged and Galway gave him a cheque in return.

Later on D Squadron's command element suffered misfortune when the 160-pounder tent which squadron headquarters used as a small mess caught fire. The complete stock of Duty Free liquor, which the officers had brought with them for the duration of the training, fuelled the flames. (Luckily Major Chiesman was able to use a QDG helicopter which he had at his disposal to replenish stocks from A Squadron.) The subsequent Board of Inquiry was invited to write off not only the tent, but also 100 tent-pegs! It was thought privately that Squadron Quartermaster Corporal 'Bert' Swaine was establishing a working surplus.

1960 saw the arrival of 2nd Lieutenants Peter Creswell, Robin Petherick, Seymour Gilbart-Denham and Hugh Van Cutsem, and the return from the Blues, where he had been attached as Equitation Officer, a post briefly revived in the early 'sixties, of Lieutenant William Loyd.

The year also saw the arrival of Brevet Lieutenant Colonel Julian Fane MC from the 12th Lancers and of Major Jim Scott from the Grenadiers. The War Office in its wisdom had decided that all future Commanding Officers were to be appointed by a selection board. If a particular regiment had no one suitable at the time, as seemed to be the case for The Life Guards after the existing incumbent had served his term, then suitably qualified officers would be posted in from elsewhere.

There was nothing new in 'imported' officers in the Regiment, Colonel Tony Meredith-Hardy and Major Derek Cooper having originated elsewhere (as for that matter had Squadron Corporal Major Eric Lloyd). Nor was there anything new in having an 'imported' Commanding Officer, although Colonel Jackie Ward had come from within the Household Cavalry.

However to post in an individual, however well qualified, at the top was hardly fair on either the officer concerned or on a closely-knit regiment such as The Life Guards. Major Jim Scott had the advantage of waiting, at regimental duty, for over three years before taking command; Julian Fane, who started life with the Glosters, did not, any more than did Lieutenant Colonel Simon Bradish-Ellames in the following decade.

The year also witnessed the start of a short-lived craze: Go-Karting. Sundays were good days on which to run races, and the large square in the 4th Signal Regiment's Hammersmith Barracks in Herford the ideal location. Major Ian Baillie was in his element, and had support from a like-minded enthusiast in the form of the Duke of Kent of the Greys who were stationed at Detmold.

When the Station Liaison Officer (SLO) came to see Baillie to complain that the civilian inhabitants of the town objected to the noise on a Sunday, the latter's characteristic reply was, 'What about their **** church bells?'

During the following year, and after the death of a participating soldier, Headquarters, Rhine Army, stipulated that all ranks taking part must carry heavy personal insurance: this effectively sounded the death-knell for the craze.

With the Saladin armoured car distributed throughout the Regiment, the crews had to be taught the art of firing the main armament. Although much of this could be achieved in the classroom or on the Field Miniature Range (FMR)* in barracks, at some point a trip to the NATO ranges at Hohne was required in order to fire live rounds.

Hohne happened to be within reach of Hamburg which, although largely razed to the ground by Allied bombing in the Second World War, was now much restored. The City-State offered much entertainment to suit every taste, more especially as the exchange rate at the time was around fourteen Deutschmarks to the Pound.

The Opera House provided first-class ballet and opera; the Four Seasons Hotel was as comfortable as any in Europe; the Emke

---

* Today known as the Classroom Instructional Module (CIM).

Restaurant, with its Victorian prints on the walls, was an especial favourite with the officers; and the Grosse Freiheit Strasse and the Winkelstrasse offered some interesting cabarets, which were appreciated by both the Quartermaster and the Padre (Rev. Robin Roe was back!) among others.

The Regiment also became accustomed to 'Quick Train'. On receipt of that code-word, abused *ad nauseam* against newly joined officers when on duty as Orderly Officer, the complete Regiment had to leave barracks within four hours ready for war and move into harbour in the countryside nearby. 'Bombing up', the loading of ammunition onto all of the vehicles, was never practised (it would have required breaking the seals on the ammunition containers), and had it been, the Regiment would never have made the time allowed.

The first time that it occurred met mixed reactions: 'Not for me, mate,' explained one trooper, 'I'm on weekend leave.' In the meantime one of the Duty Drivers was rushing around the married quarters shouting that the Russians were coming! In fact the security surrounding these turn-outs was so bad that on occasions members of the Soviet Military Mission (SOXMIS) were outside the barrack gate before the Regiment had turned out!

Towards the end of the year Major the Viscount Galway decided to retire to his estates, his place as A Squadron Leader being taken by Major William Edgedale, he in turn being replaced as Second in Command in A Squadron by the newly rejoined Captain Jan Barnes.

In the autumn of 1960 the Riding Master, Captain 'Tommy' Thompson, paid a rare visit, the War Office having agreed to the establishment of a dozen black horses with the Regiment in order to assist with the training of regular soldiers for mounted duty. These were stabled in the nearby Hammersmith Barracks and, under the day-to-day control of Corporal of Horse Nettleton, provided a great deal of pleasure for both officers and men. The Regiment bought a horsebox (from Brigadier Nelson) which enabled Life Guards to participate in the various hunter trials and shows, both military and German, that were held, and to have the odd day with the Royal Engineers' Draghounds.

Another welcome visitor was the newly appointed Director of Music, Captain 'Jacko' Jackson, together with the band. This was the first of what was to become an annual visit by the band to the Regiment while abroad. The likes of Trumpet Major Maddon, Corporal Major Kennedy, Corporal of Horse Harry Dunsmore and Musician Cox, together with the new Director, seemed to have the most incredible stamina. As well as performing concerts for the local

German towns, where they played to packed houses, there were all ranks' dances and parades, including the Remembrance Day Parade in Herford town centre.

Earlier in the year the Regiment had adopted a new order of dress. The soldiers' service dress khaki caps had given way during the previous decade to the arguably less smart but more colourful forage caps. This only applied to the Household Brigade: lesser mortals still only wore the beret.

Now, for parade purposes, in came the ceremonial white buff belt to replace the blancoed khaki belt. Battle Dress, tailored to a degree that belied its name, still had a few years to go before superseded by No.2 Dress, although ammunition boots (with studs) had been replaced for all bar the Brigade of Guards with the boot DMS (Directly Moulded Sole).

The type of drill tended to vary with the whim of the current Silver Stick. In 1960 it was standard infantry drill, though two years later, Colonel Hon. Julian Berry having taken over from the Marquess Douro as Silver Stick, it was back to forming sections with cavalry drill. This state of affairs persisted over the following ten years, A Squadron being the last to use cavalry drill for squadron parades in 1973.

Over the winter there was a change of Adjutants: Captain Timothy Gooch took a bit of leave and returned to find his cousin Captain Arthur Gooch installed in his place. The situation in barracks with three Captains Gooch was quite confusing enough, thought the other officers, without them swapping appointments as well.

If 1960 was a year of 'shaking down' with what were, for many of The Life Guards, new vehicles, guns and radios mixed with very much Second World War tactics (the Snake patrol, the box leaguer), then 1961 saw a well trained regiment taking a full part in Rhine Army activities. A 'Quick Train' which occurred during an Officers' Dinner Night nevertheless saw the Regiment leave barracks on time, waved out of the gate by the mess kit-clad Quartermaster, Captain Dennis Meakin. The annual RAC exercise against the QDG resulted in the capture of the opposition's officers' mess truck. (The luckless staff found themselves serving a meal to their captors.)

One unusual task which came the Regiment's way periodically was the escorting of nuclear convoys. This mammoth undertaking involved both escorting and guarding the American vehicles while on the move at night, and maintaining radio communications with both squadrons and Corps Headquarters, all communications being in Slidex code.

The Commanding Officer was a trifle disconcerted on one such occasion when, on entering the barn where his headquarters and their radio vehicles were situated, he found both his Adjutant, Captain Arthur Gooch, and his signals officer, Captain Simon Cooper, with a tumbler of crême de menthe set before each of them. On remonstrating with them for their intemperance, the junior officers stated both truthfully and reasonably that, since they expected to be up all night on the radio, these were their rations for the duration.

During squadron training in the spring a party of school cadets arrived to stay with the Regiment, not in itself an unusual occurrence. However, one of their accompanying 'officers' was Father Kevin Horsey, a very tall Benedictine monk. He had a partiality for cigars (in moderation), and brandy which he could happily drink all night to no apparent effect. This highly amusing and intelligent man was attached to various squadrons as they went into the field when he would place himself with squadron headquarters and, when night fell, their brandy. Father Horsey became a firm friend of Captain Timothy Gooch, now Second in Command of D Squadron, with whom he would discuss theology far into the night.

The Regiment's role in the NATO General Defence Plan (GDP) was actually practised! They deployed overlooking a small stream called the River Leine to the north of the border town of Gottingen. A subsidiary task was to help the Royal Engineers to place dummy charges under the principal bridges in the area, which was not as easy as it seemed. The radio net was jammed for a time with cryptic messages on the lines of: 'Has Holdfast put the cheeses in the mouse-holes yet?'

In August the entire 1st (British) Corps deployed for the NATO exercise 'Spearpoint'. Rather like the wartime soldier who was told a week or so after the event that he had taken part in the battle of Alamein, so it was for most Life Guards, less Regimental Headquarters. For two long weeks squadrons were tasked practically non-stop, whether it was to counter an American air cavalry attempt to seize a Weser bridge, mop up a Canadian parachute drop behind the Rear Edge of the Battle Area (REBA) or staightforward armoured reconnaissance.

The autumn also was the time that the Berlin Wall was erected. Although this, like the Iron Curtain itself, was primarily built to halt the flow of refugees to the West, the Americans reacted quite strongly. However, The Life Guards were only required to send a troop, under command of 2nd Lieutenant Hugh Van Cutsem, and an assault section, under Lance Corporal Orr, to the border at Lauenberg. Orr was widely quoted in the local German press over how much he preferred

Germany to his native Scotland, where the pubs were closed in the afternoons and there was no Reeperbahn.

Van Cutsem, a staunch Roman, had earlier in the tour once asked his squadron leader, Galway, if he could attend Mass on the following day during field training. 'Yes,' he replied, 'providing you go at sparrow-fart.' Van Cutsem spent the rest of the night looking for Sparrefahrt on his map.

Finally the Regiment decided to commemorate their 300th anniversary by commissioning from the nearby Furstenburg porcelain factory an edition, limited to fifty pairs, of china figures of a Life Guard officer in 1660 and in 1960. Captain James Rowntree, the Intelligence Officer (IO) and no mean artist, drew and painted pictures of both proposed figures, while Captain John Gooch, the only officer to speak passable German, handled the negotiations with the factory. The end result was satisfactory to all; a pair went to The Queen, as Colonel in Chief, and another to Lord Harding; a third went to the Household Cavalry Museum at Windsor, where they are still on display; while the remainder went to serving officers, who paid around £40 for the pair at the then current prices.

1962 was the end of an era — that of National Service. Obviously this had been announced well in advance, but by the end of the year the government of the day were placed in the embarrassing position of having to extend the period of service for the final drafts of conscripts by six months. For most of the year, however, the Regiment were up to strength.

Eric Lloyd took over from Eric Sant as Regimental Corporal Major, and Lieutenant Colonel Julian Fane from Muir Turnbull as Commanding Officer. Brigadier the Marquess Duoro, the former Silver Stick, became the new Commander, RAC, at Corps, conveniently as the Commander in Chief, BAOR, General Sir James Cassels, had found it necessary to impose a midnight curfew on all ranks. The Highland Light Infantry, a battalion that recruited mainly from the Gorbals, the then slums of Glasgow, had run amok in the town of Minden, causing extensive damage. From this they earned the title of 'poison dwarfs' from the Germans.

Cassels, himself from a Highland regiment, had first tried to play down the whole affair, telling a reporter from the *Daily Mirror* that it was 'a case of high spirits by the chaps'. He later had to back down and impose the curfew. Douro, apparently, pointed out that the gentlemen of the Household Cavalry could hardly be expected to be responsible for the antics of the Celtic fringe, and the curfew, for The Life Guards alone, was lifted.

That summer the complete Regiment moved down to Lake Constance (Bodensee) in the French Zone of Germany where they were the guests of the 7th Chasseurs d'Afrique and the 5th Hussars, equipped respectively with AMX13 light tanks and the ubiquitous Panhard armoured cars. (The Panhard's crew contained two drivers, one at each end, to facilitate a Gallic *volte face*.)

Since President de Gaulle of France viewed his military somewhat ambivalently at the time — he was trying to extricate France from Algeria — they were kept deliberately short of fuel so as not to encourage any march on Paris. Consequently The Life Guards had to call on the RASC for twenty-five ten-ton lorries, in addition to their own three-tonners, to carry sufficient petrol, rations and drink to sustain nearly one thousand men and over 200 vehicles for two weeks at a distance of 450 miles from base.

There was a slight language problem with the French, solved, to an extent, by the Commanding Officer, who had been on attachment in the past with the French, being fluent. On the other hand the French had an American officer with them who spoke passable English. An amusing incident happened on the night that the French held a party for the Regiment. A French Colonel decided to engage his English counterpart in conversation, so approached the most distinguished and most senior-looking officer that he could see, and started to converse in the vernacular. 'It's no use talking to me, mate,' replied Captain (QM) Dennis Meakin, who was enjoying the party. 'I don't *parly voo!*'

A token two-day exercise was held against the French who, it was found, liked stopping for lunch, which was held to be most civilized. The Life Guards were a little at a disadvantage in that the Intelligence Officer, Captain Rowntree, whose job it was, had failed to get maps of the area. This had been discovered by the Commanding Officer on the way down to the French Zone and had driven him, perhaps understandably, incandescent with rage. Over the radio rear link he was heard asking his Adjutant if he had powers under the Army Act to reduce an officer in rank summarily. (He did not.)

In fact, on the British side, the exercise was carried out by using road maps acquired from local garages and filling stations. This produced a reasonable balance with the French, who were issued with one map per troop of six vehicles.

Then it was the long haul back to Herford, staging at a United States Air Force base near Stuttgart en route. On return Brigadier Valerian Douro was again to step in to help: Major William Edgedale had been caught by the Military Police for alleged drunken driving after a mess party, and thus faced an automatic Court Martial. The Marquess informed the authorities that it was a Household Cavalry matter, so he would deal with it, as indeed he did.

The final event of note was on the sporting front: the regimental football team won the Cavalry Cup! Captain Timothy Gooch was an unlikely choice as football officer, but he gave full credit to Squadron Corporal Major Tom Gardner, the team coach.

October saw the departure of the advance party to Windsor, and the arrival of Major Johnnie Watson, a former commander of the Guards Independent Parachute Company, and A Squadron, The Blues. It also saw the departure from regimental duty, though he was to reach the rank of Regimental Corporal Major at ERE, of Squadron Corporal Major Idris Owen Jones, one of the last pre-war Life Guards. Finally the Regiment left Germany, not to return again for ten years.

Part II

THE AGE OF THE VOLUNTEER

Chapter 8

Cyrus with the
United Nations (1964)

WHEN the Regiment re-formed in Combermere in the New Year, 1963, it was only a shadow of its former self. The remaining national servicemen had been left in Germany to finish their service with The Blues, so the all-regular Life Guards, though reasonably strong in officers, were thin on the ground. Fortunately their role had been changed, together with the establishment, to that of an 'Airportable Reconnaissance Regiment'.

D Squadron were disbanded to leave two sabre squadrons (A and C), each of five troops of four Ferrets, with the command and administrative elements being confined to long-wheel-base land-rovers and trailers. These could all be fitted into a variety of different aircraft where they would be chained to the floor and flown, together with their crews, to wherever they were needed.

Headquarter Squadron were still equipped with their Bedford three-tonners (this weight referred to their capacity rather than to their overall weight) and were described as the 'Sea Tail', in other words the intention was that they would be shipped, rather than flown, to the Regiment's eventual destination.

The Life Guards also had to staff the Household Cavalry Training Squadron and Depot where all basic training for recruits to the two regiments was carried out, as well as the 'khaki rides' for those recruits heading for Knightsbridge and mounted duty. Equitation Wing training was carried out by instructors from both regiments under the control of the Riding Master, Major 'Tommy' Thompson, and was under the command of the mounted regiment.

The rebuilding of Combermere, given the final go-ahead by War Minister Jack Profumo, though far from complete, had progressed further during the Regiment's absence. The Guardroom and Main Gate had been moved from the north-east corner of the barracks to their present site further down St. Leonard's Road; 'L' block had been replaced by a new building which housed Headquarter Squadron and, for the time being, Regimental Headquarters; and Major Ian Baillie, the Silver Stick Adjutant, took great joy in commandeering the contractor's ball-and-chain crane to help to demolish 'K' block, later to be the site of the squadron offices.

The Warrant Officers and Corporals of Horse, too, had a new home, complete with an incongruous and tempting lily pond outside the main door; the Household Cavalry Hospital's days were numbered as a new 'Medical Centre' was under construction where the Guardroom had been; and the NAAFI, once a Nissen hut until it burned down, had been replaced by a more luxurious construction.

The Gold Stick came down to see the Regiment, as he had been doing regularly since his appointment. Another visitor, also a 'soldiers' soldier' like Lord Harding, was Field Marshal Sir Gerald Templer, the new Gold Stick of The Blues. Originally commissioned into the Royal Irish Fusiliers, this Great Man, a former Chief of the Imperial General Staff, was to become as popular with all ranks of The Blues as was 'Colonel John' with The Life Guards.

The year was a good one for equestrian pursuits; the polo team (Captains Ferguson, Head, Paravicini and Loyd) won both the inter-regimental and the captains and subalterns tournaments; while Lieutenant Nick Gaselee*, who was to leave in the summer after a personality clash with the Commanding Officer, had no less than eighteen rides under rules and ten in point-to-points. In March, riding Irish Jurist, he won the Grand Military at Sandown which, though restricted at that time to serving officers, attracted some fairly hot competition, especially from the line cavalry.

Militarily, the Regiment were once again back as part of the 3rd Division, commanded by Major General Michael Carver. Entering into the spirit of airportability, Captains Hon. Richard Head (his former Life Guard father had been created a Viscount for political services in 1960) and William Loyd were sent on a course on the subject at Old Sarum near Salisbury.

Part of the more basic preparations to a vehicle before loading it on to an aircraft was the fitting of condoms on to the cell filler-caps of the batteries. This was fine as far as it went. However, the army medical authorities had ceased to issue, or even to stock, these prophylactics, which was to create problems during the following year.

Both of the squadrons, in conjunction with the Royal Air Force, put the theory into practice by driving, say, to RAF Abingdon, in

---

* Gaselee, as was stated earlier, went on to become a successful racehorse trainer. His winners included Party Politics, which came first in the 1992 Grand National. By coincidence the second-placed horse was trained by Toby Balding, another former Life Guard.

Oxfordshire and being flown to RAF Lyneham, in Wiltshire, before driving back to Combermere. These exercises inevitably engendered ill-will between Life Guards and RAF personnel. On the one hand the soldiers thought that they had come to practise loading: on the other hand the RAF were damned if they were going to take to the air with any load that had been secured by mere 'Pongos'.

In June the ten-year cycle had come round for the Presentation of Standards to both regiments of Household Cavalry. Unlike in 1953, when the ceremony had taken place in the Home Park at Windsor, this time it took place on Horse Guards Parade, making use of the stands that had been erected for the Birthday Parade. Contingents from both of the regiments paraded in battledress with Ferrets, with the Mounted Regiment providing a Sovereign's Escort and the Standard Parties.

Both bands were on parade to play the appropriate regimental marches as the regiments rode and drove past Her Majesty The Queen at the end of the parade.

Later in the summer A Squadron (Major William Edgedale, Captain John Fuller, Squadron Corporal Major Smith BEM) flew, less their vehicles, to Canada. There they took over Mark I Ferrets belonging to a squadron of Lord Strathcona's Horse (the men were away on United Nation's duty in the Gaza strip) and exercised, together with the 22ieme Regiment (the Van-doos) with the 1st Canadian Infantry Brigade.

After two weeks of realistic training on the prairie in the Wainwright training area, most of the squadron made their way to Calgary in time for the world famous Stampede, before eventually flying home at the start of August. The trip was marred by the sad death, from a heart attack, of Corporal of Horse Bainbridge, a former pentathlete, in the Camp Wainwright Military Hospital.

Lieutenant Charles Harcourt-Smith and his troop from C Squadron went to Libya with 19 Infantry Brigade on Exercise 'Triplex West'. Also taking part were the Skins, a squadron equipped with Malkara missiles from the 2nd Royal Tank Regiment and the 1st Sherwood Foresters. The Life Guards Regimental Headquarters flew out as well to act as Exercise Control.

Meanwhile all was not well in Cyprus. A Squadron had been out there briefly at the start of the unrest against colonial rule, but it had been The Blues who had been in the thick of it. The Greek-Cypriot eighty percent of the population wanted the British out, a feeling which in the end was largely reciprocated, and union with Greece, which evidently was not. To this end they were prepared to go to

75

almost any lengths, which included the murders of Lieutenant Hon. Stephen Fox-Strangways, Lord Galway's brother-in-law and heir to the Earl of Ilchester, and Surgeon Captain Gordon Wilson, The Blues' Medical Officer; the latter was shot outside the British Medical Hospital in Nicosia, the capital, by Nicos Sampson, a future (though brief) president of the island.

The Turkish-Cypriots had no such axe to grind. In response to the Greek-Cypriot's EOKA, they formed a party, TAXIM, that pretended to want union with Turkey (the island had been Turkish prior to the Berlin Congress of 1878); but by and large they seemed to take the pragmatic view that life as a minority under a benevolent colonial power was probably better than that under a Greek-Cypriot majority. Owing to the difference in religions (Greek Orthodox and Muslim) there was very little intercourse of any sort between the two groups.

In 1959 the British government was forced to enter into a dialogue with Archbishop Makarios, who had been exiled to the Seychelles by Lord Harding for his active support of the terrorist cause. Then, once a form of constitution to protect minority rights had been hammered out, Cyprus became an independent republic within the Commonwealth and Makarios the first President. The British were allowed to retain sovereign rights over two military bases, Episkopi and Dhekelia, an air base at Akrotiri and the odd radio listening post. This suited everyone except for the Turkish minority.

After three years of Greek-Cypriot rule they had had enough. Over Christmas 1963 'inter-communal strife' broke out, a euphemism for the Turkish-Cypriot minority murdering as many Greek-Cypriots as they could get their hands on. This was easiest in the few mixed villages that existed on the island, and within days the Greek-Cypriot elements had all fled from these. In the towns there were fairly clear boundaries where one community stopped and the other started, Nicosia's being the 'Green Line' which was no more than a line drawn in a green chinagraph pen on the GOC's map to reflect the status quo.

Makarios had a form of National Guard and an armed Gendarmerie at his disposal, but this was beyond their capabilities: he therefore called for a Commonwealth Peace-Keeping Force.

The first of these immediately to hand were, of course, the British troops already on the island in the Sovereign Bases. Major General Peter Young, the General Officer Commanding Cyprus District, had two battalions, the 1st Glosters and the Rifle Brigade, and C Squadron of the 14th/20th Hussars on detachment from their Regiment in Libya. These he deployed, sending the Hussars to the north of the island where the trouble was worst.

Those who listened to the News in England over the Christmas and New Year break might just have heard about 'trouble in Cyprus', but in January things started to happen. As part of the Strategic Reserve, the Regiment expected that some of them might be involved. Thus it was no great surprise when, on 24 January, C Squadron were placed on seven days' notice to fly, nor that within forty-eight hours half of the squadron was airborne, the RAF having provided covers for the battery cells due to the absence of army condoms.

These were the days when, for all of the brave talk after Suez, airportability was still in its infancy. In order to move twenty-two Ferrets, eight land-rovers and trailers and ninety Life Guards over 2,000 miles in RAF Beverlys and Argosys, seventeen separate aircraft flights were needed.

C Squadron (Major Garry Patterson, Squadron Corporal Major Don Charles) arrived in Nicosia on 28 January and were met by Brigadier Roland Gibbs DSO MC, commanding 16 Independent Parachute Brigade, under whom they were to serve. Based initially at Camp Elizabeth, home for The Blues in the 'fifties, they were to relieve the Hussars in the northern part of the island and to detach a troop to the Glosters in Nicosia itself. They later moved to a Turkish orphanage on the Green Line in Nicosia.

Initially the Cypriots seemed rather appalled at the violence that they had unleashed and were quite friendly towards the peace-keepers, but this did not last long. The Greeks had a stranglehold by virtue of control of all the roads, and many Turkish villagers were in danger of being starved out. Attempts by the Commonwealth force to keep the roads open were met with increasing hostility from the Greeks, and most of the troops came under fire from one side or other at some stage. Corporal of Horse King once had to return fire with his Browning machine-gun when engaged by Turkish irregulars, while 2nd Lieutenant Victor Law had an entire Sterling magazine loosed off at him by a jumpy Greek, a tale that has lost nothing in the telling over the last thirty years.

Corporal of Horse Harding suffered the dual indignity of not only being held up at pistol-point by a Greek irregular who had jumped onto the engine-deck of his Ferret, but then to have a photograph of the incident prominently displayed in all of the newspapers. This led to the electrification of the vehicles' hulls, as had been done in Egypt in the 'forties.

Meanwhile A Squadron had arrived under Major William Edgedale, soon to be relieved by Major Ronald Ferguson, and were immediately deployed in the 'Panhandle', as the north-east part of the island was known. The Squadron Second in Command, Captain John Fuller, found himself temporarily in command on one occasion later on, and consequently went out himself to investigate an incident of some Turkish-Cypriot children being held by Greek-Cypriots.

On approaching the scene in his land-rover he came under small-arms fire. After a brief tussle with his driver over who was to occupy the bottom of the nearby ditch, Fuller walked down the centre of the road towards the gunmen, calling out 'Good morning, what a nice day!' The miscreants were sufficiently bemused to do nothing, while Lieutenant Peter Bickmore with his troop of Ferrets arrived fortuitously from a different direction.

Regimental Headquarters, having nothing left to command apart from the Training Squadron, persuaded the 3rd Division that they too were needed and came out with A Squadron, taking Headquarter Squadron, less their vehicles, as well. The only absentees, soon to catch up, were Major Ronald Ferguson, who was playing polo in Pakistan, and Capt Richard Head who was doing likewise in Nigeria.

After five moves in as many weeks, including a stay in the aptly nicknamed Goat-shit Camp, Regimental Headquarters and Headquarter Squadron finally settled in Polemidhia Camp, built by Captain Kitchener (of Khartoum) outside Limassol. They were to run Limassol District, and had under command at various times Mercer Troop, 7 RHA, a further battery of Field Artillery, B Company of the 1st Sherwood Foresters and A Squadron of the Royals, under command of Major Simon Bradish-Ellames. Later on C Squadron, once they had been relieved by the Royal Canadian Dragoons in Nicosia District after ten action-packed weeks on the island, also came under command.

A Squadron, now under the command of Major Ronald Ferguson, were fifteen miles away at Zyyi (pronounced Ziggy) and were under Larnaca District. This was controlled by the Royal Irish Fusiliers whose Commanding Officer, Lieutenant Colonel Percy Blake, established a fine rapport with Ferguson and with The Life Guards' poker players.

On the world front the problem had been raised by Cyprus at the United Nations and Secretary General U Thant had agreed to send a United Nations Peace Keeping Force (UNFICYP, not UNICEF as Captain and Quartermaster Dennis Meakin would insist on calling it) to the island. Accordingly the troops which had been deployed from within the Sovereign Bases returned to them, while those such as The Life Guards who had arrived for the emergency were joined by Canadians, Austrians, Finns, Australians, New Zealanders and the Irish.

The Irish were a delightful group, especially the 40th Battalion at

27. Submersible? D Squadron Ferret at Sohar, Oman, in 1959. *(M Austin)*

28. A Squadron (Maj William Edgedale, SCM Ron Sheffield) on the airportable establishment before returning from Germany to England, 1962. *(PR 4 Div)*

29. CoH Perkins with locals, Cyprus, 1964. (*Household Cavalry Museum*)
30. The Officers, Cyprus, 1964. Seated: Maj Ronald Ferguson,
Surg-Lt-Col Geoffrey Bulow, Lt-Col James Scott, Maj Gary Patterson.
Extreme right Lt Peter Bickmore.

31. The Officers' House, Hyde Park Barracks, viewed from the Park. The building was demolished in 1965 and is now the site of the Riding School. (*Household Cavalry Museum*)

32. NAAFI shop in Wong Padong, Borneo, in 1966. (*M Austin*)

33. Maj (QM) Dennis Meakin at the Association Dinner in 1967. (*Jay & Barral*)

34. C Squadron Officers, Borneo, 1966. *standing* 2Lt Glen McAllister, Lts Henry Boyt, Simon Hanbury, 2Lts George Thomson, David Seager (RAAC) *front* Lt Robin Petherick, Majs Simon Cooper, William Edgedale (commanding), Capt Andrew Hartigan, Lt Nigel Percy-Davis. (*Royal Marines*)

35. Maj Tony Pyman, Singapore, 1968. (*John Greenaway*)

36. Gen Michael Carver visits the Regiment in Selerang Barracks, Singapore, in 1968. *Centre* Lt-Col Ian Baillie, *right* Maj William Loyd, *behind* RCM Don Charles

37. Even in 1968 the Household Cavalry were liable to inter-service envy. (*Evening Standard*)

"Now there's real value for money on the port beam!"

38. SCM Don Turtle, Singapore, 1968.(*John Greenaway*)

39. Maj Simon Cooper, Belfast, 1972. (*Ian Kn*

40. Lt-Col Simon Bradish-Ellames, 1972. (*Ian Knock*)

41. CoH (later Capt)Andy Kelly, Belfast, 1972. Note riot stick, SLR rifle, radio, flak-jacket and helmet with protective visor. (*Ian Knock*)

42. Arms find: CoH Knowles and the Operations Officer with the largest illegal weapons haul of the 1972 Belfast tour. *(Ian Knock)*

43. 'Minor Aggro' in East Belfast, 1972. Note the size of the 'stones' that have been thrown at the patrol. *(Ian Knock)*

44. RCM Derek Stratford and Tpr Bartlett inspect an illicit still found by the RUC in Belfast, 1972. (*Ian Knock*)

45. (*below*) Maj-Gen Lord Michael Fitzalan Howard, appointed Colonel and Gold Stick in 1979. (*Household Cavalry Museum*)

46. (*below left*) Lord Mountbatten the Gold Stick, and A Squadron Leader (the author) examine a Chieftain tank in Detmold, Germany, in 1973.

Wolfe Tone Camp, Famagusta. Their armoured reconnaissance element arrived with some brand-new French Panhard light armoured cars. The hand-books for these were written in French, not a second language for the Irish, who were forced to tow the vehicles to strategic points daily while the hand-books were translated at Trinity College, Dublin.

On the sporting front the (southern) Irish challenged Lieutenant Colonel Percy Blake's Irish Fusiliers to a game of hurling, the Celtic version of football, though rougher. During play both commanding officers identified deserters from their own battalions in the ranks of the opposition teams but, wisely in the circumstances, neither pursued the matter.

The World Press Corps also arrived and lived in some luxury at the Ledra Palace Hotel in Nicosia where they would ply passing United Nations officers with refreshment. Doyen of the British was Donald Wise, then working for the *Daily Mirror*, and others included John Osman (*Guardian*) and Jack Starr (*Express*). The Hotel was on the Green Line, so it was amusing to read in the papers on the following day that 'Cyprus held its breath as fire was exchanged in Nicosia yesterday' when one knew at first-hand that an 'over' had disturbed the Fourth Estate from their slumbers by the hotel pool.

The Life Guards were obliged to amend their turnout to conform with the rest of the United Nations force. However Regimental Corporal Major Eric Lloyd, with the tacit approval of Captain and Adjutant Nic Paravicini, was damned if he was going to have his provost staff in duck-egg-blue berets and dainty scarves to match. As a concession, the United Nations' flag flew along side that of the Regiment, but the regimental police and duty trumpeter remained clad in forage caps, regimental hose-tops and buff belts. There matters would have happily rested but for the arrival in the theatre of the austere Major General Michael Carver as Deputy UN Commander to General Gyani and Commander, British Contingent (ComBritCon).

On visiting the Regiment he took a fearful view about the turnout of the staff on the gate, second only to the view that he took when the Commanding Officer and Surgeon Major Geoffrey Bulow authorized an ambulance to take two badly wounded Turks up to the Turkish sector in Nicosia. It transpired that the Turks were not only unwounded beneath the bloody bandages, but also gunmen who were wanted by the Greeks. 'You blind bloody fools!' raged Carver.

During the spring Major Jim Scott arrived to assume command and shortly afterwards fell ill and had to be admitted to the RAF hospital on the Akrotiri base where he remained for over a month. Command of the Limassol District, and for him the most important, command of the majority of The Life Guards, passed to the Regimental Second in Command, Major Toni Chiesman. This was particularly appropriate as Chiesman, after an unbroken run of nearly seventeen years with the armoured car and mounted regiments, was due to retire at the end of the year.

Cyprus, Cypriots apart, was a particularly attractive place to be at that time, as the fledgeling tourist industry was dead. Consequently service in bars and restaurants, where the men were at full liberty to go when off duty, was of the first order; both the camp at Polemidhia and that of A Squadron at Zyyi were within easy reach of the sea, as the tourist brochures would say; the beaches were sandy and deserted; and the water sports were good.

There was also a little polo for the regimental team of 1963 who were all on the island; football and cricket were played against teams from the Sovereign Bases; and the Royal Air Force, considering the scorn with which they were normally treated, were surprisingly free with their facilities in many ways.

At some point during the summer President Makarios decided to hold a party for the peace-keepers. This was handled through the office of Senor Galo Plaza (Colonel Percy Blake used to refer to him as Senor Mecca Dancing), U Thant's personal representative in Cyprus. The letter on the protocol to be observed with the Archbishop wryly intoned that it was not necessary for the guests to kiss the episcopal ring, a cause of some amusement to the soldiers. C Squadron considered sending Trooper 'Pancho' Gavan, a trouble-prone Canadian, as their representative. However, Squadron Corporal Major Don Charles vetoed that idea when Gavan was heard muttering dark threats about what he would do to the host.

Operationally the role of the United Nations was reduced to mere observer status, a fact that the natives were quick to exploit. C Squadron in general and Corporal of Horse MacKnocker in particular were constantly frustrated in their efforts to track arms convoys that went from Limassol docks up into the Troodos mountains on most nights, escorted by the Greek-Cypriot Police.

However, Captain Pyman (the Intelligence Officer) and his Intelligence Cell (Corporal of Horse Dick Bentley) were able to provide Carver with the information (from Turkish-Cypriot sources) on the names of the gun-running ships that docked in Limassol and of the return to the island of 'General' Grivas, the veteran EOKA terrorist.

Having troops out by night meant that an officer-manned radio watch had to be kept round the clock. Major Chiesman had excused himself from this chore on assuming temporary command of the Regiment. Captains Nic Paravicini and Tony Pyman thought of an ideal way to ease their burden of watch-keeping: Captain James Rowntree should be sent out from Windsor to join them, despite having attracted the soubriquet of 'Chocolate soldiers melt in the heat' from Canal Zone days. Alas, this was not to be.....

In early August the Regiment, less A Squadron, handed over Limassol District to the Royal Irish Fusiliers, packed up their blue United Nations berets (to the relief of the Regimental Corporal Major) and moved into the Dhekelia Sovereign Base Area prior to flying home. This was premature, as the Greek-Cypriots attacked the Turkish-Cypriots with some vigour in the Mansoura area in the north-west of the island. The Turkish Air Force from the mainland came to the aid of their kith and kin, and an invasion fleet sailed from the Turkish port of Iskenderun.

General Peter Young had very few forces with which to not only defend the Bases but also to evacuate the many dependents who lived outside them, should the threatened invasion occur. The scare soon lifted (the invasion was carried out for real some years later) so, two weeks later than they had planned, the main body went home. They left behind Corporal of Horse 'MI5' Brown and his driver, Trooper McCumiskey, killed when their Ferret went off the road in the mountains, and later to be joined by 2nd Lieutenant Patrick Gordon-Smith from A Squadron whose Ferret turned over on the Limassol to Zyyi road. They were all buried with full military honours in the British cemetery in the Dhekelia Base.

Every squadron leader who has an independent command, given half a chance, will run it as a private army. Ferguson was no exception with A Squadron. Well liked by his men, possessing a determined streak and what his Second in Command referred to as a Superiority Complex, Ferguson ran a relaxed but efficient team at Zyyi. The squadron had its own water-skiing boat and camp cinema; with no less than eight officers under his command which, together with redoubtable Squadron Corporal Major Jack Smith BEM, meant that there was plenty of time for relaxation; and he persuaded General Young, who had earlier told him to remove the self-designed pennant from the bonnet of his land-rover (it went well with his own trumpeter, Corporal McQueen) to hold a dance for his officers at Government House.

When the Turkish invasion threatened, Ferguson deployed his troops around the Turkish-Cypriot villages in the area, which earned the squadron effusive thanks from the villagers for protecting them. Little did the poor villagers know that the United Nations forces had received express orders not to intervene in any way in the case of an attack on the villages, only to observe and report back!

The squadron was also required to run C Squadron's Ferrets to the port at Famagusta for shipment back to England. This they did, handing them over to an RCT port officer before returning to Zyyi. Two were stolen that very night, apparently by Greek-Cypriot irregulars, which caused a considerable fuss, though nobody could blame the squadron.

Come the end of October the advance party from the 1st Cheshires arrived to take over from the Fusiliers, shortly to be followed by Major Geoffrey Duckworth and Captain Frank Golding of Ajax Squadron, 2nd Royal Tank Regiment who were to relieve A Squadron. This was done in some style by Ferguson who, though strong on man-management, was weaker on administration. He therefore assembled what can only be described as a Brains Trust team, comprising his key squadron headquarters personnel together with Sergeant Dick Tracy of the LAD, Corporal of Horse Bill Johnson (MT, or 'Daimler Hire' to the squadron) and Corporal Walsh, the squadron's Master Cook.

The team managed to field all of the technical questions posed by Duckworth bar one: the location of the village of Zyyi's Muhkdar (Head man). It later turned out that he was working in the Officers' Mess kitchen! The farewell party somehow involved Captain Golding being thrown out of the window; then the squadron flew from Akrotiri to Lyneham in Wiltshire on Guy Fawkes Day, and went on a month's leave. They had been away from their families for eight months.

Chapter 9

The Far East and
the Bamboo Curtain (1966-1968)

1965 SAW the small Regiment together again and a great number of changes of personnel were to take place over the next eighteen months. First and foremost was the new Gold Stick. A sailor might not seem to be a logical choice as Colonel for a regiment of heavy cavalry, but when the sailor is Admiral of the Fleet Earl Mountbatten of Burma, currently Chief of the Defence Staff and 'Uncle Dickie' to the Royal Family, the logic becomes apparent.

Not that he was unknown to the Regiment anyway. He had been attached to the 2nd Life Guards in 1921; the Commanding Officer had served on his staff as an ADC in India; and, as the father of modern polo, he had given Ferguson a lift to Pakistan to play the game in the previous Spring.

Major Toni Chiesman had departed over Christmas. Like Majors Ronald Ferguson, John Fuller and latterly James Hewitt, command eluded him through his inability to pass the written side of the examination for promotion to substantive major. This was a *sine qua non* for onward promotion to Lieutenant Colonel in the peacetime army, let alone attending the Staff College. This in no way detracted from their value as regimental officers – rather the reverse. By spending nearly all of their service with the Regiment they provided a continuity that the soldiers liked, and which was missing to an extent from the more ambitious career officers.

Major (QM) Dennis Meakin moved to Knightsbridge, his place being taken by Captain (QM) Eric Sant, the last man in the Regiment to wear the Warsaw Mermaid on his uniform, having served with General Anders' Polish Corps in Italy during the Second World War. Also on the move was Regimental Corporal Major Eric 'Bunker' Lloyd: after twenty-seven years of service, literally as both man and boy, he went into retirement. Many was the tale told about him, mainly apocryphal, e.g. Lloyd at a mess meeting: 'There's no point in buying a candelabra — nobody can play the damned thing!'; Lloyd to the barber, who had asked him how he would like his hair cut: 'Bloody fool — same as yesterday!'

His son, John, carried on the tradition eventually retiring, also after extended service, as a Regimental Corporal Major Instructor in Kuwait. Together father and son had over fifty years of loyal and exemplary service as Life Guards. Mr E.O. Lloyd RVM is currently an active member of the committee of the regimental association.

By a narrow majority the Town Council decided to confer the Freedom of Windsor on the Household Cavalry, which naturally involved a suitable parade to commemorate the honour. This distinction was rather lost on the contingents from the mounted regiment: one of the periodic epidemics of equine 'flu confined the horses to barracks, so the men had to march up Castle Hill on foot!

Elements of both sabre squadrons exercised in Libya during 1965 and were also much in demand to show off their airportability skills. The Regiment were still part of the 3rd Division, now commanded by Major General Cecil 'Monkey' Blacker OBE, MC, a showjumping former 'Skin' who was later to become Adjutant General. As Household Troops the Regiment were still inspected annually by the Major General Commanding the Household Brigade, the incumbent at that time being Major General John Nelson DSO, OBE, MC, who was shortly to become GOC Berlin.

The polo team was still active and were the losing finalists in both the inter-regimental and the captains and subalterns tournaments; and Major Ronald Ferguson, then Vice Chairman of the Household Brigade Polo Club, ran a polo course for young army officers.

Captain Tony Pyman had a fine time in point-to-points riding Captain Hon. Richard Head's horse, Beau Caprice, which either fell or won on every occasion. In fact this truly remarkable horse in its time performed in almost every equestrian discipline except for polo. As it was a black horse, Head had it taken on strength as his charger at Knightsbridge and also used the horse as a hunter at Melton Mowbray; Corporal of Horse Boris Thompson (brother of the Riding Master) evented it; and to cap it all Beau Caprice, the oldest horse in the field, won the Gloucester Hurdle at Cheltenham with Tommy Jennings up.

Finally at the end of the year, after 305 years of training their own recruits internally, the Household Cavalry Training Squadron, under the newly promoted Major Tony Pyman, were moved to the Guards Depot, Pirbright. It is not the purpose here to open old wounds three decades later, but this was highly controversial since the entire Regiment, less officers and attached personnel, had at that time been trained at Combermere. The system might not have been as slick as that at 'Woodentop Farm', but it had worked well. (Twenty-five years on, the rumour that the Guards Depot might be closed as part of the Defence cuts fills all ranks with horror!)

In the new year Captain Seymour Gilbart-Denham became Adjutant (his cousin, Captain Loyd, was at the time Adjutant at Knightsbridge) and Don Charles the Regimental Corporal Major. Later in the year the Riding Master, Major Walter 'Tommy' Thompson DCM, went to Melton Mowbray, as Chief Instructor, after thirty-three years with the Household Cavalry, his place being taken by Captain Alec Jackson.

Towards the end of 1965 the Regiment had been warned for duty in the Far East, *terra incognita* for The Life Guards, for the following year. So in the spring of 1966 Lieutenant Colonel Sir James Scott Bart, as he was now titled following the death of his father, went out to reconnoitre the likely locations for his squadrons. The flag had not yet been hauled down on the British Empire, though the socialist government were shortly to announce the phased withdrawal of all commitments 'East of Suez'.

The Japanese had occupied all of the European colonies in the Far East during the Second World War. However, their surrender after the atomic bombs had been dropped at Nagasaki and Hiroshima had meant that the colonies had been re-occupied peacefully.

Hong Kong island (Victoria) and the littoral part of Kowloon opposite had been leased to the British during the previous century in perpetuity by the Chinese after the rather shameful Opium Wars; while the remainder of Kowloon and the New Territories, an area of land roughly equivalent to Yorkshire, were (and are) due to revert to China in 1997 at the end of their leases. (The conservative government of the 'eighties decided to hand all of the colony back at the same time.)

While Hong Kong remained a Crown Colony, Malaysia, a federation of the Malay States, had been granted their independence in 1956 during the 'Communist Emergency'. The former anti-Japanese fighter, Chin Peng OBE, and his Chinese gangs sought to drive out the British and the traditional state rulers by terror in order to install their own regime. This was thwarted by the firm leadership, coupled with a 'hearts and minds' policy, of General Gerald Templer.

Singapore, under the single-minded and London-trained lawyer, Lee Kuan Yew, had left the federation early on and decided to become independent; and Brunei, sandwiched between Sabah and Sarawak in Borneo, had not joined anyway. The majority of Borneo was Indonesian, formerly a Dutch possession, and it was not long before their President Sukarno started the period of 'Confrontation'. This involved sending troops across the border into Malaysia and Brunei. Fortunately the British had enough troops, including Gurkhas and the fledgling Malaysian Army, to repulse the incursions which had virtually ceased by the time that The Life Guards arrived in the theatre.

Back at Windsor the Regiment had a manpower problem. Though recruiting for regular soldiers, largely run at the time by Major Christopher Wordsworth, was good, it was not sufficient to expand a two-squadron airportable recce regiment to a three-squadron armoured car regiment at a stroke. B Squadron was optimistically re-formed, only for A Squadron to be disbanded and The Blues to be asked to provide a complete squadron, to be commanded by Major Jim Eyre of The Blues, to become 'Blues Squadron, The Life Guards'.

Junior officers also were in short supply, even with The Blues Squadron providing their own. As a result Lieutenants Dick Morrisey-Paine, Christopher Going and Captain Christopher Churton were posted in from the line cavalry for the duration. Morrisey-Paine later transferred to The Life Guards, eventually commanding at Knightsbridge. Two Australian subalterns were also posted in, though that was routine policy for the theatre.

After a farewell ball at Combermere, attended by The Queen, the Regiment went by coach to Heathrow to board chartered aircraft, the modern troopships, for the Orient. (For the first time all ranks and their dependents had to carry passports, the officers and soldiers being described as on 'Government Service'.)

Mr Harold Bamberg, at the time the owner of Eagle Airways and a polo-playing friend of the Regiment, had arranged for the band to be allowed onto the tarmac, and for the VIP Kingsford Smith Suite to be available for the officers. (A bill was later received for the food and drink consumed in the Suite, largely due, said the officers, to the presence of Captain Simon Crisp of The Blues!)

On arrival in the Far East Regimental Headquarters and B Squadron (Major Timothy Gooch) went to Paroi Camp near Seremban on the western side of the Malay peninsula, C Squadron (Major William Edgedale) and the (helicopter) Air Squadron went to Wong Padong Camp in Sarawak (the 'k' is silent), Borneo, and The Blues Squadron went initially to Nee Soon camp and later to Selerang Barracks, next to Changi Jail, in Singapore.

An Air Squadron was something that had been long promised to armoured car regiments, possibly as an inducement to persuade them to release officers for pilot training. Now at last The Life Guards had one, their trained pilots being Captains Charles Harcourt-Smith and Tom Hickman, together with Captain Christopher Haworth-Booth, who had transferred from the Royals, and Corporal of Horse Skyring. These were supplemented by Captains Peter Salter and Thursby Lang, from the line cavalry, and commanded firstly by Major Hon. Peter

Lewis of the 15th/19th Hussars and then by Major Peter Stonor of the Queen's Own Hussars.

But perhaps the most colourful character of them all was Corporal Digney. Having started his military career as a smooth-talking national serviceman in charge of the Hyde Park Barracks telephone exchange in the 'fifties, he had rejoined as a regular and eventually ceased his service in the 1987 as Corporal Major in charge of the Officers' House in Combermere.

On this occasion he was a sort of 'Mr Fix-it' with the Air Squadron, though firmly ground-based. He was most recently seen at Eton's 550th anniversary celebrations in 1990 where, as a front-man for Searcy's, the caterers, he was greeting his former officers.

The Regiment were followed out to the Far East by an old friend: Lieutenant General Michael Carver arrived, firstly as Commander, Land Forces, and later, as a full General, as Commander in Chief. Later in the tour the General paid an official visit to the Regiment, including a statutory visit before lunch with the officers, to the Warrant Officers and Corporals of Horse Mess.

'What would you like to drink, General Sir?' enquired Regimental Corporal Major Don Charles.

'Nothing,' replied Carver, a teetotaller.

This cast a slight dampener on his visit to the mess: it was felt he could have put the members at their ease had he wished by asking, say, for tomato juice, as even The Life Guards' Corporals of Horse had heard of abstainers, even if they had never met any.

On a more serious level, there was bound to arise the question of what to do if a soldier wished to marry a native girl in the Far East. This was not racist but impractical: there was hardly any social contact with local people, bars apart, so the sort of girls whom the soldiers met were hardly the sort to take home to meet mother. The Regiment's slightly paternalistic method of dealing with this was to post the soldier to one of the other squadrons for a few months, which usually did the trick.

If not, no further obstacle was placed in the couple's way. Major John Fuller, as he was to become, remembers a soldier's Chinese wife a year or so later when the Regiment was in Germany asking him how to obtain a German Highway Code written in Cantonese!

One group of people, usually from the Indian subcontinent, who did very nicely indeed with the British Army from Cyprus to Singapore, were the contractors. The likes of Mahommet Ali, Taj Dhin and Kushi Mahommet were but some of those who served the Regiment well, normally undercutting the NAAFI with their 'Wog

Shops', and being able to provide, or knowing a chap that could, anything from a belly-dancer to a sharkskin dinner jacket at short notice.

The Blues Squadron in Singapore were the recipients of nearly all of The Life Guard recruits that were drafted out to the Regiment. By early 1967 there was a predominance of Life Guards, so when Major Tony Pyman took over from Major Jim Eyre, the squadron reverted to being A Squadron, The Life Guards, once again. Since most of the men were newly joined, it did mean that the squadron which went to Sharjah two years later was almost unchanged, thus very efficient.

Selerang Barracks, which along with Changi Jail had been used by the Japanese to house 17,000 allied prisoners in the Second World War, were truly palatial. The great barrack blocks with their wide verandahs and high ceilings with electric fans remained relatively cool, while the servants' quarters of the officers' houses were larger than some quarters at home.

A generous Local Overseas Allowance (LOA) enabled married officers to employ labour — a kebun (gardener), amah (cook) and ayah (nursemaid) were considered to be the ration for a captain, who would pay their wages himself. The Ministry of Defence provided an amah free for married soldiers and single men had a variety of competing boot-boys who would clean their kit.

The enormous camp area around the barracks contained all of the normal sports facilities, and since the Regiment worked 'Tropical Hours', there was plenty of leisure time to indulge in outdoor activities. One of the three air bases, RAF Changi, was next door also, with its Officers' Club, library and so forth. It was also where the new VC10 RAF transport planes were based for eventual carriage home.

Singapore City, about half an hour away by car, contained some very fine restaurants and hotels (the Goodwood, Raffles [named after Sir Stamford Raffles who acquired the island for the East India Company in 1819], the Cockpit and the Troika, to name but a few). It also contained all manner of bars and brothels, coyly referred to by the Military Police who patrolled them (it was an offence to enter them) as 'houses of assignation'.

An amusing diversion in barracks over a period of around a week was the filming of Leslie Thomas's book, *The Virgin Soldiers*, starring Hywel Bennett and Lynn Redgrave. Although no soldiers were allowed to take part, many of the wives obtained lucrative employment as extras.

Armoured-car training, as opposed to individual trade training, was impossible on the island, about the size of the Isle of Wight and heavily populated. To practise tactics, or to fire the 76mm Saladin guns, it was necessary to drive past the huge Naval Base (home of the British Far East Fleet) and over the causeway into Malaya.

Regimental Headquarters, Headquarter Squadron and half of the Air Squadron soon moved down to Selerang Barracks from Seremban to come under the command of 99 Gurkha Brigade, itself part of the 17th Division. C Squadron, soon to be commanded by Major Desmond Langley, returned from active service with 40 Commando, Royal Marines, in Borneo to Seremban with the other half of the Air Squadron.

C Squadron had the usual ration of war stories, though these were on the lines of the time that the nervous sentry put an entire magazine through the roof of the Officers' Mess, or fishing with grenades while on river patrol with Lieutenant Simon Hanbury's 6 Troop. In any event they qualified for the General Service Medal with a 'Borneo' clasp.

B Squadron (Major Arthur Gooch was shortly to take over as squadron leader from his cousin) had meanwhile been sent up to Sek Kong Camp near the Chinese border in Hong Kong's New Territories.

Soldiering with armoured cars in Malaya was a fairly relaxed affair. Chin Peng was believed to be still alive and living quietly near the border with Thailand, and the occasional party of SAS operated in the deep jungle in that area. The vehicles of course were useless in both primary and secondary jungle which covered the mountains in the centre of the peninsula, and the only Assault Troop in the Regiment, under the command of Lieutenant Christopher D'Oyly, passed from A Squadron to B Squadron.

However, the troop was under command of Major (Timothy) Gooch's B Squadron at Paroi when the squadron were invited to lay on a demonstration of ambush clearance for the divisional commander, Major General Gordon Patterson DSO, OBE, MC, a keen Gurkha. A small column would be mock-ambushed; the escorting Saracen Armoured Personnel Carrier would disgorge a section; and they would dive into the jungle, only to reappear quarter of a mile further on shortly afterwards charging the ambushers.

Major Gooch decided on a little stage management at this stage, as it would take the section up to an hour to cut their way through the jungle. A further section was therefore concealed in the jungle just short of the objective, and it was to be these who emerged shortly after their fellows had gone in further down.

It all went well in rehearsal, but caused slight embarrassment on the day when the General decided to go in with what he believed to be the assaulting section.

Other moments of drama also tended to be comical rather than tragic: the Commanding Officer, by this stage Lieutenant Colonel Ian Baillie, under the impression that the pilot of the helicopter was reading the map, neglected to do so himself. Captain Hickman, the pilot, had not, so they had to put down in a paddy field for the night, lost. Then there was Lieutenant Dick Morrisey-Paine who awoke in his bivouac to find a snake around his legs; and finally Corporal Major Johnnie King and the tiger.

King had been sent on foot to the top of a jungle-clad hill to act as an overnight signals relay station. (Communications after dark in the tropics were dreadful.) At around midnight he called up to calmly inform control that he was being stalked by a tiger. There was, of course, absolutely nothing that anyone could do to help him, and he, of course, had no live ammunition for his rifle. The former SAS soldier held his nerve, and the tiger eventually departed.

There was, however, an extensive network of roads and laterite tracks around the enormous rubber plantations that covered most of the flatter land near the coasts and were suitable for training. Interestingly the rubber tree was not indigenous to the area, but was imported from South America towards the end of the nineteenth century. The plantation managers were always very friendly, mindful of recent troubled times, though the Europeans were being phased out in favour of local men.

One of their local watering-holes was the Sungei Ujong Club near to Paroi Camp and straight out of Somerset Maugham. Sweaty planters in shorts would jostle at the bar for the ubiquitous Tiger beer, taking time out to ogle the odd Malay wife or consort. The club had tried to remain all white on Independence. However, Templer had threatened to deport the whole committee unless they changed their policy.

Malaysia being tropical, malaria was prevalent. It was an offence to catch the disease which would indicate that the individual had not swallowed his daily Paludrin pill. Strangely Singapore was meant to be malaria-free. However, all ranks took the pills because constant trips to the mainland rendered them at risk. Other disorders included monsoon blisters, prickly heat, gastritis and a variety of social complaints, all dealt with by Surgeon Lieutenant Colonel Geoffrey Bulow and his staff. At one point there was an outbreak of cholera among the Singaporeans — not altogether surprising considering the appalling smell from the mangrove swamps and the inadequate drainage.

What the Americans at the time called 'Red China', as opposed to the only bit that they recognized, Generalissimo Chiang Kai Shek's regime in Formosa, was going through a convulsion in the form of the 'Cultural Revolution'. Though their enormous army could have overrun Hong Kong and the nearby Portuguese colony of Macao within a very short space of time, they contented themselves with fomenting civil unrest.

In Macao this was a great success: after a time Portugal told China that they were leaving. The riots stopped and the Portuguese were allowed to stay, but very much on Chinese terms.

Matters were quite peaceful when B Squadron arrived in Hong Kong. They were quartered with 48 Gurkha Brigade, the officers having to conform to the Gurkha habit of having breakfast (always mulligatawny soup) when British soldiers normally were enjoying their mid-morning NAAFI break. The brigade commander, Brigadier 'Bunny' Burnett, gave the officers a crate of the soup at their leaving party at the end of the tour to remind them of an occasion when they had come in to breakfast after Battle Fitness Tests only to find that the soup was 'off'.

The squadron also had to take their turn at providing the Guard at Government House. By tradition this was always formally inspected by His Excellency once during a tour. Corporal of Horse Bruce Payne, Guard Commander, stood with his men at ease outside Government House awaiting the arrival of Sir David Trench, expecting an immaculate figure in a white uniform with a feathered hat.

Instead he saw some sort of minor diplomat clad incongruously in shorts, an open-necked shirt and a Trilby hat emerge from the building, but it was not until his squadron leader bellowed from the crowd watching, 'Carry on, Corporal Payne!' that the penny dropped: HE's formality did not match that of his Guard.

Large-scale riots started in the city in early 1967, which were contained with great courage by the locally enlisted Hong Kong police and their British officers. The city was placed out of bounds, much to the annoyance of Captain John Fuller, who had recently arrived from Knightsbridge with expectations of 'Eastern Promise'.

Fuller in fact was in temporary command of the squadron when the police post at the border crossing at Sha Tau Kok came under armed attack from China in July. With five dead and thirteen wounded the police called for military help. The 1st/10th Gurkhas with B Squadron under command advanced on the beleaguered post, with Lieutenant Peter Bickmore's troop in the van. Bickmore himself came under accurate machine-gun fire but, conscious of his orders of not escalating matters, did not return the fire. Having reached the objective, he had to remain there for a further three hours while the Gurkhas dug in and the casualties were evacuated.

Bickmore received The Queen's Commendation for Brave Conduct. It was fully deserved, yet reflected a sign of the times: ten years previously Cornet David Blake of The Blues had been fired on in Cyprus, had promptly returned the fire and had shot a terrorist. He was Mentioned in Despatches. Now the award was for not returning the fire, though to have done so could have caused unthinkable repercussions or a posthumous Victoria Cross!

Meanwhile the Mounted Squadron had been taking part in the filming of The Charge of the Light Brigade at Aldershot!

The war between the Communist North Vietnam and the American-backed South Vietnam in former French Indo-China was rising towards its zenith at around this time. (Major William Edgedale, now Second in Command, spent a spell in Saigon as Assistant Military Attaché during the period.) Both Hong Kong and Bangkok were designated as Rest and Recuperation (R&R) centres and descended to meet the challenge of entertaining the US armed forces with a will. Hong Kong had a head start as they used (Hong Kong) Dollars which tended to become confused with the American 'green-back' when bills were presented.

Towards the end of the tour Captain and Adjutant Seymour Gilbart-Denham's allotted time was up (usually two years) and he handed over to Captain Robin Petherick. He had been responsible during his time in the Far East for starting *The Acorn*, the highly successful regimental magazine which has been produced annually ever since.

After a final farewell cocktail party in the Officers' House in Selerang (Donald Wise, now in retirement, was one of the guests) it was time to hand over to Colonel Robin Carnegie and his Queen's Own Hussars.

The Commanding Officer decided to make his own way home. Marriage had put an end to his motor racing, so he had taken up flying. To this end he had bought a single-engined Cessna (9M-AMR) with which he used to terrify his various officers with amusing stunts such as flying over virgin jungle on an empty tank, or threatening to cross the Java Sea when the plugs were clearly oiling up.

Wisely taking Squadron Leader Sam Key of the RAF with him, but so overloaded that the watching officers were betting as to the likelihood of it failing to take off at all, the little plane taxied past the assembled VC10s and giant Hercules transporters to take off in a northerly direction. Needless to say he had an uneventful journey.

In November, 1968, the Regiment came home to Combermere,

together again for the first time in two and a half years. The officers were amused to hear shortly afterwards that the Hussar officers had been banned to a man from the RAF Officers' Club in Changi within two weeks of their arrival!

Chapter 10

Ulster and Elsewhere (1969-1971)

BEFORE the Regiment had left the Far East, news had been received of the impending amalgamation of The Blues and the Royals. 'Couldn't happen to a better bunch of blokes!' muttered an unfeeling Corporal on hearing the news from the Commanding Officer in the cook-house. The Regiment had not felt at risk, relying on the 1922 amalgamation of the 1st and 2nd Life Guards to keep them inviolate on this occasion.

The deeper implications struck home when they re-formed in Combermere in 1969 for The Blues, under Lieutenant Colonel Mark Darley, had only moved as far as Perham Down (near Tidworth, Hampshire) where they were converting to an armoured role. The end of nearly thirty years of armoured reconnaissance for both regiments was at hand. The heavy cavalry were reverting, perhaps, to their traditional role.

Another change, which had been phased in over the last few years, was the replacement of all regimental cooks by men from the Army Catering Corps. This at the time was thought to be a retrograde step, nevertheless the new cooks under WO II Pete Howard provided the superb catering for February's Household Cavalry Warrant Officers and Corporals of Horse Ball at the Lyceum in London.

There was a change in role also for C Squadron: under the enthusiastic Major James Emson, who had transferred from the Parachute Regiment two years earlier, they became part of the Allied Command, Europe, (ACE) Mobile Force. For the next two years they would disappear for lengthy periods, either to freeze in Volvo Sno-Cat vehicles in Norway or to catch the sun in their Ferrets on NATO's other flank in Turkey.

A Squadron (Major Loyd had taken command at the end of the previous year in Singapore) went to Denmark and Schleswig-Holstein as part of Brigadier Peter Leng's 24th Infantry Brigade for the aptly named NATO exercise Bold Adventure. Gales in the North Sea ripped off the bow doors of the LSL (thereafter it had to complete the journey to Esbjerg stern-first) and twenty degrees of frost made the exercise most memorable.

On return the squadron were warned for a nine-month unaccompanied tour in Sharjah, one of the Trucial States in the Persian

94

Gulf and last visited by the squadron ten years previously. Squadron Quartermaster Corporal Derek Stratford became Squadron Corporal Major on the retirement of Squadron Corporal Major Don Turtle, and his place was filled by Staff Corporal Dick Bentley.

The time had come for a routine change of commanding officer: Lieutenant Colonel Desmond Langley took over from Ian Baillie, the latter becoming Silver Stick. Many were the tales told about 'Toad' Baillie, most of which today would be described as sexist. Others dwelt on his Scottish parsimony, or on his particular sense of humour. Nonetheless this well-loved officer's heart was always with the Regiment, and after he was killed in a traffic accident nine years later (driving to Colonel Sir Robert Gooch's memorial service), the Guards Chapel was packed to capacity for his service. (He also left in his will a large sum of money to regimental funds.)

The situation in Northern Ireland began to get ugly over the summer: the republican Roman Catholic minority became increasingly embittered by what they perceived as oppression and discrimination by the Protestant 'loyalist' majority. B Squadron (Major John Fuller), being the only ones left, were notified that they might have to go to the Province, however were allowed to proceed with preparations for an exercise in France. Lieutenant Christopher Joll was orderly officer on the weekend that the summons came. Acting on instructions, he informed the Palace (apparently The Queen had not been amused when The Blues had been sent off somewhere without Her being told on an earlier occasion), Lord Mountbatten, who was on holiday in Ireland, the Commanding Officer and Squadron Leader. He then had to start calling back the men.

There appeared to have been no contingency plans for reinforcing the garrison in the Province in the event of inter-communal violence. The Regiment were to find themselves committed piecemeal over the next eighteen months in aid of the civil power, before being deployed, with proper notice and training, as infantry in Belfast in 1972.

On this first emergency tour, B Squadron drove to Marchwood where they embarked (with difficulty — the bow doors would not open following an accident) on the LSL *Sir Geraint*. Once at sea neither the captain of the ship nor the squadron leader had been told where in Northern Ireland they were to go. Eventually they put into the military port of a largely burning and looted Londonderry and the armoured cars were off-loaded on Mexeflote pontoons.

Awaiting them on the quay was a senior officer, dressed in the full uniform of the North Irish Horse, who instructed them to carry out a Flag March down to the 17th/21st Lancers in Omagh, which was right up Major Fuller's street after his experiences in Mukalla. Thereafter the squadron, which lost their Saladins early on as 'looking too aggressive', filled a variety of roles which included patrolling the Falls Road with, amongst others, the 1st Hampshires, to prevent the Catholics being murdered by the feared B Specials (since disbanded, but then part of the Royal Ulster Constabulary [RUC]).

Christopher Joll particularly remembers the food in the Territorial Army mess, where they were finally billetted, as being so disgusting ('I, personally, will never eat heart again.') that Fuller took a holiday cottage, sent for his wife and dog (emergency tours were officially unaccompanied by either) and set up a home at which his, and visiting, officers were welcomed.

Joll also remembers that Lieutenant Hon. Johnny Astor took a weekend off to go shooting with The Queen at Balmoral. He was apparently closely quizzed by his Colonel in Chief on the situation in Her Province.

If Corporal of Horse Anderson was the first of the Regiment's casualties (gun-shot wound in his arm from a 'loyalist' in the Shankhill Road), then Lieutenant Bill Grandy was the first serious casualty. He and another soldier were searching a car from opposite sides when the cocking handle of the other's light machine-gun snagged and then went off, sending several bullets into Grandy. He very nearly died, and needed extensive blood transfusions over the next few weeks, some of which came from the men in his troop. This led to some typical black humour on the lines of 'Of course officers don't have blue blood. It's red, same as ours.'

B Squadron were home by Christmas after a four-month tour. Major John Fuller moved to Knightsbridge for his third and final tour, his place being taken by Major Timothy Gooch MBE who had spent two years as Silver Stick Adjutant. His decoration was due to some high diplomacy over the amalgamation of The Blues and the Royals or, as he succinctly put it at the time: RHG + Royals = RHG/D + MBE.

Since A and C Squadrons were still otherwise occupied in, respectively, Sharjah and the ACE Mobile Force, it was again B Squadron who prepared for an exercise in France during the summer; again it was B who were warned for Northern Ireland one Saturday when they were all on leave; and it again was B who were, less two men, deployed within twenty-four hours.

Initially they went to Long Kesh camp, better known today as the Maze prison with its H blocks. Later they were quartered in Gosford Castle, then with the 17th/21st Lancers in some comfort. At one point they spent an uncomfortable night in a disused railway cutting when the officers' mess truck, and more importantly its sustaining contents, got lost. 'One or two of the officers had to drink water for the first time since leaving Eton,' commented Joll.

Shortly after their arrival, Regimental Headquarters and C Squadron followed. The latter were detached for duty in Belfast, while the former went to Long Kesh.

The so-called Irish Republican Army (IRA), who had been around since 'The Troubles' half a century before, were now starting to exploit the situation: though the British Army had initially been seen by the Catholics as saviours, hatred was being whipped up among them to regard the soldiers as brutal oppressors. This sometimes led to a subconscious bias, no more, against the Catholics from the men.

The IRA had just started to make their presence felt in Londonderry and in West Belfast, and indeed on the border with the Republic of Ireland. Though the border was well marked on the major roads, it was often less than clear on the minor roads, which led to map-reading errors. Major Timothy Gooch at one point had to confess to the Commanding Officer that his entire echelon had strayed some miles across the border. A land-rover and several 3-ton trucks are not easily overlooked, and Gooch preferred that Lieutenant Colonel Desmond Langley heard it first from him.

He was surprised to receive no reprimand: furthermore Colonel Desmond admitted, rather sheepishly, that he had done the same with Regimental Headquarters only days before, only noticing his error when he espied a green, rather than red, pillar-box.

A Squadron, in the meantime, were completing an interesting, if monastic, nine months in Sharjah. They were under the operational command initially of Brigadier Roland Gibbs as part of Land Forces, Gulf, whose Headquarters were in Bahrein. Administratively they were controlled by Colonel Kenneth Timbrell CBE, MC, a former Royal and one of the last great Arabists. The camp, which was shared with the RAF, had been thoroughly modernized, on Mountbatten's orders, from what the squadron had encountered ten years previously and now boasted air-conditioning, swimming pools, sports facilities, cinemas and so forth.

Sharing a camp with the RAF presented no particular problems as the cultural divide between the two services was deep enough in those days to cause voluntary non-fraternization in both directions. It was a squadron of the Queen's Own Hussars a year before who, amongst other amusing digressions, erected a large sign on the boundary where the army stopped and the 'Boys in Blue' started. 'Attention!' proclaimed the sign, 'You are now entering a non-saluting area.' The sign stayed up for several days before Colonel Timbrell had it removed.

The Sharia (Muslim law) was not enforced to the extent that foreigners could not consume alcohol in the privacy of their own camp, nor worship their own God with their own Holy Men — indeed the Ruler of the State of Sharjah even allowed a tiny cemetery for British dead within the camp perimeter. There was, however, no contact with the local population beyond the Squadron Leader attending a *Fudl* (feast) with Sheikh Raschid of Dubai, the neighbouring ruler. The Arab women were not only clad from head to toe in black, but also were compelled to wear a leather face-mask.

In Oman, though continuing to employ British officers, such as Colonel Peter Thwaites of the Grenadiers, to command his troops, the despotic Sultan Said bin Taimur ensured that lepers and the blind were still in abundance. His presence proved so embarrassing for HMG that they inspired a near bloodless coup shortly afterwards, installing his Sandhurst-trained son Qaboos in his place, much as had been done earlier with Sheikh Shakbut in Abu Dhabi.

The squadron undertook a Flag March around the northern half of the country (there was a lively communist insurrection in the mountainous south) and were totally resupplied by air-dropped or air-landed rations, fuel and mail. Water was drawn from the ancient water-courses or *falajin*, to which was added purification powder. Corporal of Horse Fettes was the only survivor of the climb of the Jebel Akhdar, and on this occasion he was taken to the top by one of the helicopters that accompanied the squadron.

Apart from the Flag March in Oman, the squadron spent their time in patrolling the seven Trucial States, and going on exercise with the 1st Queen's Own Highlanders whose commanding officer, Lieutenant Colonel Andrew Duncan, had been Brigade Major when the squadron had been in Singapore. The Highlanders were later followed by the 1st Scots Guards under Lieutenant Colonel Murray de Klee.

For those who wished to live dangerously, Captain Charles Harcourt-Smith, one of the two captains in the enormous squadron of 112 all ranks, would arrange amusing diversions: these included marching across desert and mountain from the Persian Gulf to the Indian Ocean, or climbing the Jebel Hafit, a vertigo-inducing mountain near the Buraimi oasis on which some Cameronians had perished in earlier years.

Sharjah was also a great place for VIPs to 'drop in' providing that they were not required to stay out in the sun for too long. Apart from the expected run of the Major General (Hon. Michael Fitzalan

Howard), the Silver Stick (Colonel Ian Baillie) and the Commanding Officer, Government Ministers Roy Hattersley and Ivor Richard both visited the squadron.

Major Andrew Hartigan came out to take command for the last three months. He was accompanied by 2nd Lieutenant James Ellery, who had recently lost his driving licence (speeding), so had been posted to a place where one was not needed. He was attached to the troop of Lieutenant Peter Rogers, a former Royal, now Blue and Royal, who had volunteered for the tour. Rogers was one of the the better troop leaders in the squadron which included other experienced troop leaders such as Lieutenants Peter Fletcher, a former Blue, and Andrew Imbert-Terry.

After nine months in the desert the squadron returned in July, 1970, to Combermere. Captain Morrisey-Paine had become Adjutant and Regimental Corporal Major Charlie Rodger was nearing the end of his term. Recent arrivals had included 2nd Lieutenant Anthony De Ritter from Sandhurst, and some of the new Scorpion tracked vehicles which were planned as replacements for the ageing Saladins.

The main emphasis was now on conversion to armour, specifically the four-man Chieftain tank. Most of the Regiment attended courses at either Bovington, Lulworth or Catterick, and in March, 1971, B Squadron (Major Arthur Gooch) departed for Lothian Barracks in Detmold, West Germany, to join The Blues and Royals as the advance squadron of The Life Guards. Elements of the remainder of the Regiment took part in exercise 'Battle Royal' in Long Valley, Aldershot, which was a demonstration of tactics old and new by the Household Division for their Colonel in Chief. Major John Fuller's charge at the head of the Mounted Squadron, with swords drawn, was one of the more impressive displays!

In the autumn the rest of the Regiment went to Germany. Lieutenant Colonel Desmond Langley was succeeded in command by Simon Bradish-Ellames, a former Royal. Derek Stratford became Regimental Corporal Major, taking over from Jim Morris who was commissioned as Motor Transport Officer.

By the time that they were settled in their new home and anticipating coming to grips with their new role in the 1972 training season, they were warned for duty in Belfast as infantry on an emergency tour instead.

Chapter 11

Belfast on Foot (1972)

'Ride, Drive and Fly with the Household Cavalry' read the recruiting poster in the 'sixties. No mention was made of being deployed on foot in the slums of East Belfast, yet that is what the Regiment, in 1972, were required to do.

They had been to the Province before and they were to go there again, but the first and only time that they went to an urban setting in the infantry role is worthy of note.

For a start there was the question of who was eligible to go: those under the age of eighteen and those with any form of Irish connection were not. Thus Corporal Major Kit Juleff's Ulster-born wife meant that he was ineligible, so he went on attachment to Uganda instead. (The 'Irish connection' ruling was in order to protect the families concerned, rather than from any fear of unreliability from the soldier.)

The 'Irish connection' ruling was to be modified in later years, but on this occasion it caused so many men to remain as the rear party that C Squadron, the 4th/7th Royal Dragoon Guards (Major Raymond Layard, Captain Simon Jenkins), joined the Regiment for the duration as the third squadron to bring the strength up to that of an infantry battalion. Within the Regiment the eligible soldiers were re-formed from the three sabre squadrons into two 'rifle squadrons' (No.1, Major Arthur Gooch, Corporal Major Les Lumb, and No.2, Major Simon Cooper, with former Blue and Royal Corporal Major Stan Deaville) which in turn contained three troops of six half-sections each. Each squadron had a small command element and an echelon, while Regimental Headquarters was to be split into 'Tactical' and 'Main'.

Headquarter Squadron (Captain Tom Hickman, Corporal Major Lawrence Gibbs) would continue to function much as normal, however the LAD would stay in Germany to overhaul all of the tanks during the four-month tour. In addition the Regiment had to find an Intelligence Cell (Captain John Bedells, Lieutenant Bill Jones, Corporal Major Ken Whalley and Trooper Bartlett); an Operations Officer (Major William Loyd); a Press Relations Officer (Captain John Gill, also to be the editor of the monthly magazine for the Regiment, *The Blue Light*); and a mobile regimental reserve, 6 or Special Troop

(Lieutenant James Ellery). Finally six men were to be detached for plain clothes duty with the Mobile Reaction Force (MRF).

Then there was the training. All ranks had received basic infantry training up to platoon level when they were recruits, but in the case of those more senior, it would have been a few years before. The officers, too, well versed in Duties in aid of the Civil Power, or 'Tactics C', were fully capable of marching a body of armed troops towards a mob of rioting (and unarmed) natives of a darkish hue, sounding a bugle and unfurling a banner stating 'Disperse or we fire' in the vernacular. Now, these drills were suddenly obsolete.

The Ministry of Defence, shaken by the killing of thirteen rioters by men of the Parachute Regiment in Londonderry earlier in the year ('Thirteen dead from Army lead' read the wall graffiti in the Catholic areas), had started a Rhine Army Northern Ireland Training Team to which the Regiment repaired. Living in Staumühle camp on the edge of the Sennelager training area and with Foot Guard sergeants instructors attached to each squadron, Major John Baskervyle-Clegg of the Grenadiers and his team patiently taught The Life Guards all of the refinements learned from the experiences in the Province to date.

The Mark I 'Tin City' had been erected on the training area, a mock-up of an urban street in scaffolding and corrugated iron in which the troops could practise riot control. They also learned about house searches, body searches, vehicle searches and the setting up of Vehicle Check Points (VCPs).

They spent time doing 'pokey drill' with the SLR rifle to get accustomed to holding it pointing skywards whilst on patrol for a matter of hours; they spent hours on the ranges firing their weapons; they filled sandbags to build sangars; and Sergeant Scriven of the Grenadiers taught them Aikido. Towards the end of their training the squadrons returned in turn to Lothian Barracks where the Operations Officer and the Regimental Corporal Major had laid on a very realistic exercise for them, using the rear party and the wives as Belfast citizens. (Corporal Major Joe Miles's wife, Betty, was universally held to be far more dangerous than anything that might be encountered in Belfast!)

Finally the Recce Party flew to Belfast where they saw for themselves East Belfast for which they were to be responsible. Their briefing from Major Peter Graham of the Gordons, brigade major of Brigadier Frank Kitson's 39 Infantry Brigade under whose command they would be coming, was as good as that of the staff officer from Headquarters, Northern Ireland, was bad. The Engineer regiment, whom they would be relieving, were in rather low spirits as they had lost a Staff Sergeant to a terrorist bullet shortly before. He had been shot, in typical IRA fashion, as he was helping to construct a playground for the Catholic children of the area — a Community Relations project.

The Regiment moved to the Province in July and were responsible for the whole of East Belfast, predominantly Protestant and quiet at the time, in general, and for the small Catholic enclave, known to the locals as Short Strand, in the Ballymacarrett district, in particular. To give an idea of scale, the Catholic area was about 500 yards square.

Since the IRA had declared an open season on British soldiers, there was no question of anyone walking out when off duty, and when on duty not only were they all armed, but also dressed in American flak jackets and carrying steel helmets with visors, respirators and riot sticks. Since also, both in theory and in practice, the Regiment were on duty twenty-four hours a day, all ranks were restricted to two alcoholic drinks per day. Since the only supply was through squadron canteens this was easily enforced, and in fact some chose to go 'on the wagon' for the duration.

Communications between half-sections and squadron operations rooms were by portable Pye transceivers, similar to those carried by policemen today; and the final item on the inventory was the Federal Riot Gun, another American import, from which were fired rubber, and later plastic, bullets. Much has been written about plastic bullets which could and did cause death if fired at close quarters. But when used correctly, they had a deterrent effect on a rioting crowd when the only alternative would have been CS Gas, held but rarely used on orders from above, or real bullets, Parachute Regiment style.

Regimental Headquarters (Tac) and Nos.1 and 2 Rifle Squadrons were billetted in, respectively, Mountpottinger police station, two church halls and a flea-infested bus station in Ballymacarrett; C Squadron 4th/7th RDG eventually were settled to the south in Castlereagh; and Headquarters (Main), 6 Troop and Headquarter Squadron lived in comparative luxury in the now-vacant prison ship, HMS *Maidstone*. Although the ship had no engines, she had not been decommissioned, hence boasted a captain, a navigating officer and crew!

The aim of the Army's presence in the Province was to stop the two communities from harming each other while the politicians 'worked something out' to the satisfaction of both sides. Twenty-three years after the first troops were committed that is still the situation. Early in 1972 Westminster imposed direct rule in the Province by suspending the Ulster internal parliament at Stormont, yet the year was to be the worst on record with a total of 467 deaths attributed to violence.

The Army operated under the provisions of the Special Powers Act, which also sanctioned Internment without trial for suspected terrorists, both Protestant and Catholic.

The main factions with whom the Regiment had to contend were the republican Provisional IRA, a proscribed organization in the Province, whose aims were for destabilization in the short term, and for a United Ireland under a form of Marxist rule in the long term; and the loyalist Ulster Defence Association (UDA), then a legal organization, though their methods became increasingly similar to those of the IRA, whose broad aims seemed to be to return to the *status quo ante* with the Province being run by the Protestant Unionist party. Both of these organizations had splinter groups over which they had varying degrees of control.

Shortly after the advance party's arrival in July there occurred 'Bloody Friday': twenty-two IRA bombs exploded in Belfast killing thirteen people (including two Welsh Guards) and injuring 120 others. A 200 lb bomb in No.1 Squadron's area was defused by an Ammunition Technical Officer (ATO) from the truly brave bomb disposal squad of the Royal Army Ordnance Corps.

On the following day the regiment were treated to the usual 'baptism of fire' that greets any newly arrived unit. Seventy-eight shots were fired at Life Guards, all missing. (Corporal Major Whalley, who was on duty in the sangar on the roof of the police station, claimed that his flak-jacket was struck.)

A week later the Regiment left Brigadier Sandy Boswell's 39 Infantry Brigade and, together with the 1st Welsh Guards (Lieutenant Colonel Michael Lee) who controlled the city centre, came under command of Brigadier Kenneth Perkins' 24 Airportable Brigade. This was part of the massive build-up of troops to around 22,000 for Operation Motorman.

The Catholics in Londonderry had erected barricades around their sections of the city which had been allowed to become 'no-go' areas to the security forces. The Protestants in Belfast, and in particular those in the Dee Street area, which was part of No.1 Squadron's territory, had done the same. It was clearly unacceptable to have places in the United Kingdom in which the forces of law and order could not go, so at four o'clock in the morning on 31 July all the barricades, both Protestant and Catholic, were seized and, with Royal Engineer help, removed. That, in brief, was Operation Motorman.

The next major problem, two days later, was after a gunman from the surrounding Catholic area shot and wounded two workmen in the Protestant Sirocco factory in Ballymacarrett. A strike was called, vehicles and buses were used to block many of the roads in the Protestant areas of East Belfast and the enormous workforce from the nearby Harland and Wolff shipyards marched on Short Strand. 42 Commando, Royal Marines (Lieutenant Colonel Jeremy Moore) and 25 Battery, Royal Artillery, (Majors Keith Wilby and Tony Bianco) came under command, as did a company of Queen's Own Highlanders. This large force ensured that the Sirocco men could get in to work on the following day without the dubious assistance of a reputed 2,000 UDA men, who were beginning to appear for the first time in paramilitary uniform.

Two weeks later the situation had quietened sufficiently for the last troops still under command to be released. However, the Regiment were required to turn out twice a day for the remainder of the tour to line Mountpottinger Road when the factory's workforce arrived and left.

Taking advantage of the slight credit accumulated with the Catholics due not only to this but also from the rubbish clearance carried out by Life Guards during a dustmen's strike, the operations officer managed to persuade the Royal Ulster Constabulary to take to the Catholic streets again, from which they had been absent for some months, with The Life Guards. The Regimental Corporal Major later organized regular RUC/Life Guard patrols, and he also persuaded the bus company to resume driving and stopping on routes in the area.

At the start of September the UDA let it be known that they had 'had enough' and were withdrawing cooperation. On the following evening heavy rioting was started by the 'Tartan' gangs of young Protestants and Willowfield RUC station came under attack (repelled by the police firing buckshot). At some stage the operations officer came across a pleasant-looking young man scribbling in a pad, while rubber bullets, bricks and bottles flew around him. He identified himself as Robert Fisk, the *Times* man in Ulster. Other press reporters, who paid a brief visit to the Regiment, were Simon Winchester, then with the *Guardian*, and Martin Bell of the BBC.

A further welcomed visitor, who was literally passing through on his way back to England after an active spell in Londonderry with his Ferret squadron, was Major Andrew Parker Bowles of The Blues and Royals.

After about a week of Protestant rioting, looting, arson and the odd sectarian murder during which some sixty baton rounds (plastic bullets) were fired and rifle fire had been exchanged, what passed for peace returned. By the end of September, 24 Brigade Headquarters went home to England, the Regiment reverting to 39 Brigade.

October started badly. Lance Corporal of Horse Leonard Durber, who was attached to the MRF, was fatally injured following an incident with the UDA near their headquarters in Newtownards Road. He died, the Regiment's only fatality, four months later without regaining consciousness, leaving a wife and two young children. This, coupled with the murder of a member of the undercover force by the IRA on the previous day, led to a reappraisal of the whole concept of the MRF.

UDA trouble flared again during the following week. 6 Troop under the Operations Officer (Lieutenant James Ellery was enjoying his mid-tour three days of leave) had a large arms find when they searched the Oval football ground. Thereafter the troop was out continuously over the next twenty hours as Protestant gangs fired on both Regimental Headquarters and No.1 Squadron's base and once again put Willowfield RUC station under siege. 142 baton rounds were fired, mainly by No.2 Squadron and by 6 Troop, and five soldiers were injured, including Corporal Marshall who had to be sent back to hospital in England.

In the following week the UDA 'ceased cooperation' again, and the night of 16 October can only be described as one of action. With help from C Company,1st Royal Green Jackets, and 25 Battery RA, nearly 600 baton rounds and seventy-two rounds of rifle fire were expended to leave four rioters as certain deaths and the area pacified. Eleven soldiers needed hospital treatment, four with gunshot wounds, while a further twenty needed first-aid treatment.

A form of Mad Hatter's Tea Party took place three days later, when the Commanding Officer entertained UDA 'officers', such as Frankie Jones and Sammy Tweed, to tea at No.1 Rifle Squadron Headquarters, he in turn being entertained at the house of the UDA commander, Tommy Herron. (Lieutenant Ian Knock, Royal Signals and the largest officer in the Operations Room, went along as bodyguard, suitably clad with a shoulder-holster.) The promises of peace from the UDA leaders were shattered on the following day when Lance Corporal Creighton and Trooper Welton were both wounded by the same bullet fired at them in a Protestant area.

Shoulder-holsters had also become required apparel for officers attending Rev. Ian Paisley's church of the Christian Martyrs, not that a fire-fight was anticipated during worship or on consecrated ground. Since they had to be in uniform, they were easily identified and were singled out for praise earlier in the tour: 'We welcome the gallant members of the security forces.' After the UDA troubles the Reverend rounded on them as the 'spawn of the Devil' and 'three prongs of evil', so attendance dropped off.

To say that nothing really happened for the rest of the tour would be simplistic. Incidents, be they shootings, bombs or bomb hoaxes, house searches and foot patrols still continued, as did the static duties of manning the sangars and Observation Points, Vehicle Check Points and Key Point guards. It was also the season of large Protestant marches, whose organizers would invariably pick, and be given police permission for, routes that would pass along the interface with the Catholic area. The interface also had to be guarded every morning during termtime to prevent the inhabitants of either community from hurling abuse and more at the children of the other who were on their way to school.

A very trivial issue that aroused some heat during the tour was that of the cakes baked for the soldiers by Dear Old Ladies. These cakes tended to be delivered to HMS *Maidstone*, and the suspicion from the outposts was that that was where they stayed. Reports, which at times would escalate to squadron leader level, would come in that the pay sergeant, say, had been seen on *Maidstone* with a complete cake on his desk. The local joke at Regimental Headquarters (Tac), which was entirely without foundation, was that the chief culprit was Major Tony Pyman, the Second in Command, who was based on the ship.

Though the senior ranks led very much from the front, with high profiles in their particular areas, in many ways it was very much a Lance Corporals' war, as that was the rank of a great many of the commanders of the half-section patrols. The Commanding Officer , Lieutenant Colonel Simon Bradish-Ellames, was subsequently awarded the OBE and Regimental Corporal Major Derek Stratford the MBE, and all ranks felt that they had earned their campaign medal.

Perhaps a suitable epitaph was one which came inside a Christmas card to the Regiment when they were back in Germany:

> To the very gallant men of The Life Guards who looked after our district. . . Sincere thanks and hope that you enjoy Christmas with your loved ones. Many of us miss you and your cheerfulness in the face of what you sometimes had to put up with, but most of our people thank you, boys, for giving us the comfort of your presence and keeping us safe at night from both terrorists, IRA and UDA. . .

> From one of the many moderate Catholics.

Part III

THE AGE OF THE PROFESSIONAL

Chapter 12

Detmold with Tanks
(1971-1975, 1980-1984)

THE conversion to armour and the move to Detmold in 1971 signified, for The Life Guards, the end of an era. Uniquely the Regiment had held the role of armoured reconnaissance in some form for thirty-one years and consequently had developed a high degree of skill in it, in particular map-reading, radio communication and speed of reaction.

Now not only were new skills needed to match the new era, those of coming to terms with the highly technical machine that was the Chieftain tank, but also a totally radical outlook on, for want of a better word, soldiering. For the Rhine Army of the 'seventies was considerably more professional than that of the early 'sixties, and there was no room for those who failed to adapt, although most made the transition.

For a start there were the Germans themselves. In 1962, when the Regiment had last served in the Federal Republic, only two officers (Captain John Gooch and Lieutenant Hugh Van Cutsem) spoke more than a handful of words of German. The locals all learned English as a second language, so there was really no need. Now, although they still learned English, they seemed to expect that the visitors on their soil should make some sort of effort to communicate in the vernacular, however hesitant. Most Life Guards made an effort.

Their army, the Bundeswehr, now had teeth in the shape of the fast Leopard tanks, while their Air Force had American Starfighter jets. (Since these latter fell out of the sky on a regular basis, it was a questionable blessing at best.) There was a new air of self-confidence in their armed forces, who were not bedevilled by the 'Guilt-Cringe' of their left-wing intellectuals.

Then there was the money. Although the LOA was generous and drink, cigarettes and petrol were duty-free, the pound that fetched thirteen Deutschmarks ten years before now only achieved eight. The country was rich: the menu in the town's main hotel, the Detmolder Hof (where officers could have the bill transferred to their mess-bills) was of West End standards.

On the subject of money, the time had come for the retirement of the Paymaster, the former gunner and prisoner of war of the Japanese, Major 'Chev' Wilmot. This well-liked officer had been with the Regiment for a full eleven years. No high-tech man he, his accounts were done with the aid of an abacus and small scraps of paper in the cash-box, and he was once heard to ask if his losses could be offset against tax!

His departure coincided with the decision to pay all of the soldiers in future by variable credit direct to a local German bank. After initial confusion for those who had not hitherto held a cheque-book, and therefore thought of them as licences to print money, the system worked; and it thereby saved the two hours of a Thursday which had previously been allocated to squadron pay parades.

Drink and drunkenness, always a problem when a great many young men are together in an alien environment and action is not imminent, had been a problem in BAOR since the Second World War. From the German pubs on pay-day, the NCOs' messes after 'happy hours' and the officers' messes after drinks parties, in all of which it was considered machismo to consume, and hopefully hold, quantities of alcohol, men from all ranks would climb into their cars and kill themselves in traffic accidents.

After years of exhortation, action was taken. The Military Police, who had full powers over soldiers and their dependents within Germany, emulated, then surpassed their civilian equivalents in Britain with the use of the breathalyser; tales were told of men being dragged from their baths in their quarters to be tested, and it was an automatic trial by court martial for those found positive. These draconian measures, although increasing the dislike for the 'Red-caps', were effective, to the enrichment of the German taxi firms. Many will remember Herbie*, whose taxi was the saviour of many Life Guards who felt the need to leave their cars where they had dined.

But most important of all was the change, for the Regiment, in military thinking. No longer 'Corps Troops', who would turn up when required and then disappear again afterwards, the Regiment was now an integral part of 20 Armoured Brigade, together with the 9th/12th Lancers and 1st Royal Horse Artillery, both of whom were in the neighbouring barracks, and the 1st Light Infantry in nearby Lemgo. The Life Guards went to their parties and they came to Life Guard parties. The Brigade was commanded by Brigadier Richard Lawson

* Herbie is currently running a fleet of taxis in the Detmold area and was recently approached by the former East Germany and asked to advise on setting up taxi firms there.

47. The Queen, with Lt Hugo Fircks *(left)* and Lt-Col James Ellery, inspects the Airborne Troop on Smith's Lawn, Windsor Great Park, in 1989.

48. Maj Simon Falkner with Brig Arthur Gooch (Commander, RAC Centre) in 1989. Behind: Capt Christopher Mitford-Slade and Maj Christopher Anderson. (*J Ellery*)

49. Olympic Pentathlete Capt Dominic Mahony with ex-King
Constantine of the Hellenes at the 1989 Inter-Services event. (*J Ellery*)
50. Operation 'Trustee': Lt David Waterhouse commands his Scorpion
on security duty at Heathrow airport in 1978. (*Press Association*)

51. The QM(Tech) Troop at Soltau, 1973. *(standing)* 2nd from rt, Capt (QM) Jim Greaves, *(seated)* CoH Shortman, RQMC(E) Bill Johnson, LCoH Harrison.

52. Winners of the Inter-regimental polo tournament, 1979: Capt Peter Hunter, 2Lt Charlie Graham, Lt Iain Forbes-Cockell, 2Lt James Hewitt with the Colonel *(centre)* and the Royal Navy team on Smith's Lawn. *(Mike Roberts)*

53. Belize: Lt James Astor commanding his Scorpion.
54. After a day with the Weser Vale Bloodhounds: Capt Dominic Mahony, Lt James Gaselee, Maj James Hewitt, Lt Rupert Uloth. (*J Ellery*)

55. Sovereign's Escort in July, 1986, on the occasion of the wedding of Prince Andrew to Sarah Ferguson: Lt-Col Seymour Gilbart-Denham rides on the right wheel of the carriage which contains The Queen and Maj Ronald Ferguson. (*Mike Roberts*)

56. Officer of the 'nineties: Lt Mark Hanson, Cambridge graduate and Pentathlon Blue. (*J Ellery*)

57. Gulf Battlefield Replacements: Capt (QM) Chris Slater, RCM John Belza, Lt-Col Anthony De Ritter, Capt Hugh Robertson, Capt Nick Garrett, 2Lt Martin Rees-Davies, Saudi Arabia, 1991.

58. Challengers and Chargers: Maj James Hewitt surveys the options, Saudi Arabia, 1991.

DSO, who had also been decorated by Belgium and the Vatican for his incredible bravery in the Congo (Zaire) ten years earlier.

Lip-service had been paid in the past to 'infantry/tank cooperation': now the two armoured regiments, the gunner regiment and the battalion formed three Battle Groups which in turn split into Combat Teams. A Squadron on a brigade exercise, for instance, could lose a troop to 1LI, gain a platoon instead and be able to call on gun-fire, in theory at least, from Chestnut Troop, 1RHA, the battery located with the Regiment.

The troop of army black horses had been re-established in the time of their predecessors, The Blues and Royals, and were to continue through to the Union of the two regiments in Windsor in 1992. The stable was run by Staff Corporal Dick Batey, a former Knightsbridge farrier, with great efficiency. It was also complementary to something that had not been seen in Germany for twenty years – a regimental pack of hounds!

The Weser Vale Bloodhounds, a three-quarter-bred pack, had been formed in Detmold in 1969 by Captain (QM) Bill Stringer of The Blues and Royals. They hunted the natural scent left by a soldier-volunteer runner over German farm-land, for which permission had been obtained in advance and on which some fairly solid obstacles had been erected. The Corps Commander, Lieutenant General Sir Roland Gibbs, was a regular follower, as were a handful of Germans, together with as many Life Guards of all ranks for whom the stable could supply mounts. Wives were eligible to ride army horses. However, only one hunted regularly at that time, and she was Austrian-born. The remainder contented themselves with 'wives rides' under Corporal of Horse Sherwin, attached from The Blues and Royals.

Since the two regiments of Household Cavalry continued to alternate between Germany and Windsor up until 1992, when the hounds were given to a syndicate of German enthusiasts, there was Household Cavalry continuity with the pack for twenty-three years. Hounds were hunted on the arrival of The Life Guards by Major Christopher Haworth-Booth, a former Master (as was Major Arthur Gooch) of the Eton Beagles. His normal mount was the black horse Sefton which was so badly wounded in the IRA bomb outrage outside Hyde Park Barracks in 1982.

The Regiment were based in Detmold with Chieftain Tanks for the following thirteen years, albeit with a five-year interval at Windsor between the two tours. The first tour, during which the Regiment were desperately trying to become familiar with their new role, was highlighted by the two regimental emergency tours in Ulster (the first of which was described in the previous chapter). There was also the 1973 Presentation of Standards in London; and a regimental Battle Group went twice to Suffield, in Alberta, Canada, where the tank training facilities on the joint Canadian-British base, recently opened, were unrivalled.

It is to the credit of the Commanding Officer that, despite the difficulties in coming in to command from outside mentioned earlier, as the only officer with tank experience he cajoled, persuaded and drove the Regiment into becoming good tank men, despite everything else that was taking place at the time.

The Presentation of Standards followed much the same format as that of 1963, with both regiments being on parade with their mounted squadrons and a Ferret squadron each. This meant that C Squadron reconverted to Ferrets and drill with the Stirling SMG for the parade and, more importantly, the Commanding Officer, as a former Royal Dragoon, had to be taught how to ride on a ceremonial parade.

Lieutenant Colonel Simon Bradish-Ellames OBE was a willing pupil who was soon to be seen trotting around barracks with his stirrups crossed in the best cavalry tradition. He even took a black horse up to Soltau during troop training, his trumpeter following with a man-pack radio. It was a pity, thought Spanish speakers, that he insisted on the call-sign 'Tonto One'.

At this point the Regiment received a new medical officer in the form of Surgeon Captain Charles Goodson-Wickes. He was a hunting man as was Surgeon Major John Stewart, his predecessor, who now moved to Knightsbridge, and indeed as had been Surgeon Captain Anthony Page of The Blues and Royals. Goodson-Wickes was only to spend a few years with the Regiment before leaving to go into politics. However, he reappeared as a volunteer medical reservist in the Gulf campaign of 1991, the only Member of Parliament so to do.

During August, 1973, after a period of squadron training at Vogelsang (a welcome change from Soltau), Regimental Headquarters, itself now part of what was called Command Squadron, A Squadron, Chestnut Troop, 1RHA, C Company, 1st Royal Irish Rangers, and 3 Troop, 39 Field Squadron, Royal Engineers flew to Calgary via Newfoundland. They then embussed for Crowfoot Camp, Suffield. At Calgary A Squadron veterans of Cyprus nine years earlier were greeted by ex-Trooper Gavan, complete with Cadillac, who had clearly prospered since the days when his stoppages exceeded his pay.

Crowfoot Camp and the surrounding prairie produced a sense of *déjà vu* for those of the squadron who had been in Sharjah four years before. Sun-compasses were available, and used, and a crash course in the location of the Pole Star enabled the squadron to navigate by night. After shaking down, the Battle Group's live-firing battle runs, some of which took all day and involved negotiating mine-fields, were certainly the most realistic training that the Regiment was ever likely to encounter before A Squadron's crossing of the berm into Iraq eighteen years later.

Suffield, the history of which was covered in a book written in the 'eighties by Brigadier James Emson, was an area of around 900 square miles of undulating prairie. The nearest town was Medicine Hat which is on the South Saskatchewan River and, coincidentally, held a Stampede during the Regiment's stay. Four mounted dutymen from the Regiment paraded at the start of each session for which numerous free tickets were made available in return.

After the training was complete, all ranks dispersed over the North American continent for a few days' leave before flying back to Germany. There followed numerous changes and promotions due to postings and retirements. Lieutenant Colonel Simon Cooper assumed command in December, 1973, with Captain James Ellery as his Adjutant; Majors Seymour Gilbart-Denham and Charles Harcourt-Smith became squadron leaders; respectively, Captains Howard Schotter (a future Russian Orthodox priest who had just returned from a posting in Brunei) and Anthony De Ritter were their seconds in command; and Major James Emson became the Second in Command of the Regiment.

In January, 1974, 2nd Lieutenant Philip Metcalfe went absent, taking his sleeping bag to the value of £14.46 with him, and has been absent ever since. An Oxford undergraduate and a subaltern in Ulster in 1972, he nonetheless had expensive habits which exceeded his pay. Word later came from Major John Scott of The Blues and Royals, who was at Saumur, that Metcalfe had joined the French Foreign Legion in approved style. His departure was not mourned by his brother officers.

Also in the New Year various Ferrets, Saracens and land-rovers appeared on the square: the Regiment was due for Ulster again, this time as 'Mounted Infantry'. A compressed visit was made to Hohne (the Regiment received the coveted A grading for their gunnery), during which the Guided Weapons troop indulged in live firing for the first time (100% success with the first salvo!). They then moved to Soltau for troop training before much the same pre-Ulster training took place again as had been carried out two years before. An Assault Troop was once more formed, commanded on this occasion by Lieutenant Paul Hearson.

Initially the Regiment were stationed, on their arrival for the summer of 1974, in Gough barracks, Armagh, and were responsible for forty-five miles of the border and fifty-four crossing points with the Irish Republic. To assist them in this task they had under command B and C Companies of the 1st Green Howards, respectively responsible for the towns of Armagh and Dungannon, and a company of the 1st Duke of Edinburgh's Royal Regiment at Aughnacloy.

Then, for varying periods, also under command were Tiger Company, 4th Royal Anglians, a battery of Marine Artillery, a troop of Royal Scots Dragoon Guards and elements of the Royal Military Police. Three platoons of the 1st Parachute Regiment were also attached for patrols on the border. Swathed in belts of machine-gun ammunition, they appeared very warlike, but tended to give more trouble in Gough barracks than out in the countryside.

Later No.1 Squadron was to be attached to 7 Parachute Regiment, Royal Horse Artillery in Newry, Newcastle and Newtownhamilton. This last outpost, as chance would have it, was commanded by Captain Simon Falkner, on detachment from the Regiment to the Guards Independent Parachute Company, who had commanded a troop in No.1 Squadron in Belfast two years previously. Finally the troops of Lieutenant Hon. Nigel Adderley and 2nd Lieutenant Jeremy Harbord came under command of the 1st Grenadiers in Londonderry. The Life Guards were over 1,000 strong and twelve different cap-badges were being displayed at various times.The enormous Regiment was part of 3 Infantry Brigade, commanded by former Coldstreamer Brigadier Colin Wallis-King.

The Regiment had patrols, both mounted and dismounted, which crisscrossed their area, searching derelict barns and woods; close observation patrols were mounted for days at a time, all with the aim of reducing the IRA's ability to operate.

In the middle of June Staff Corporal Hutchings, with a section from Captain Charles Horsfall's troop, arrested eight terrorists and recovered weapons and bombs in Eglish. Later in the month was the start of the so-called 'proxy' bombs whereby terrorists would hold an innocent man's family as hostage to persuade him to drive a bomb into a military base or outpost. 3 Brigade's response to this was to order holes (Critpits) to be dug in the various camps and barracks into which proxy bombers should hopefully drive their vehicles. This was done, but luckily was never put to the test with the Regiment.

The usual ration of VIPs called on the Regiment, including Major General Philip Ward, now commanding the Household Division, and who had had A Squadron under command towards the end of their

Sharjah tour five years earlier, and Major General Peter Leng MC, the Commander, Land Forces Northern Ireland.

The Regiment returned in September with as many Life Guards as when they had set out and reorganized as an armoured regiment for the third time in as many years. With a back-log of nearly nine months on which to catch up, it was back to Soltau for troop training. A change which had taken place during the Regiment's absence was a considerable increase in security in all barracks. From now on all cars were stopped at the barrack gate, be it Combermere or Lothian barracks, and the driver invited to open his boot and bonnet.

Before the year ended there was the annual Fitness for Role inspection, carried out by Major General Michael Gow, a former Scots Guard; the newly commissioned Lieutenant (LE) Don York arrived from Knightsbridge to take over from Captain (LE) Jim Morris as Motor Transport Officer; and Lieutenants Hon. Robin Cayzer and Hon. Gilbert Greenall took fifteen soldiers on a Free-Fall Parachuting course at Sennelager.

1975 was another year for change as it marked the reconversion from armour to armoured reconnaissance for the Regiment. First, though, was the usual firing at Hohne, with a pitiful amount of ammunition for the tanks and none for the guided weapons, followed by troop training at Soltau. To an extent this was also pre-Canada training for the Regiment who, less C Squadron, were due back at Suffield in June. C Squadron, under Major Tim Earl, recently transferred from the King's Own Border Regiment, went off to Norway to join up with a squadron of The Blues and Royals in preparation for joining the ACE mobile force again on return to Windsor.

A late thaw caused the abandonment of much of the training in Suffield, though it provided another opportunity for all ranks to explore North America. C Squadron, after getting suitably cold in Norway, were the first to start conversion for their new role; the Regiment won almost all of the prizes at the annual Rhine Army Summer Horse-show, including that of the most successful horse of the show, which went to Widow, ridden by Major Tony Goodhew.

Finally, in October,1975, the Regiment came home to Windsor after four very turbulent years.

In February, 1980* , Lieutenant Colonel Arthur Gooch took the Regiment back to Detmold with Captain and Adjutant Simon Falkner and Regimental Corporal Major Andy Kelly. Majors Nick

* The period from October, 1975, to February, 1980, is covered in Chapter 13

D'Ambrumenil and Christopher D'Oyly commanded A and B Squadrons (and were also joint-masters of the Weser Vale Hunt); Majors Charles Harcourt-Smith and James Ellery, recently returned from a staff appointment in Oman, C Squadron and the revived D Squadron; and Major Anthony De Ritter returned from Headquarters Household Division to command Headquarter Squadron.

Major Jim Morris and Captain Les Lumb, the Quartermasters, had replaced, respectively, Majors Don Charles and Jim Greaves; Captain (LE) Bruce Payne had replaced Captain Don York as Motor Transport Officer; and Captain (LE) Derek Stratford MBE had retired during the previous year after twenty-five years of service with the Regiment.

The barracks were much the same as before. However, the establishments had changed. At regimental level there was no longer a recce troop, guided weapons troop, nor a command squadron. This enabled the Regiment to find the manpower for a fourth sabre squadron, though initially thirty Blues and Royals were retained in Detmold until the Regiment was up to strength.

At higher level the Ministry of Defence had decided to dispense with Brigades in Germany during the previous decade. Thus the Regiment, though still a part of 4th Armoured Division, were split between two 'Task Forces', each commanded by a garrison commander. Typically the majority of the Regiment came under command of a task force based around Minden, though based in Detmold garrison. This extraordinary experiment was abandoned a few years later, and the Regiment reverted to being under command of 20 Armoured Brigade in 1983.

The tour started sadly due to the untimely death from a heart-attack of Surgeon Major Kevin Connolly*. This charming man had not enlisted until the age of forty and had come to the Regiment after a spell with the 1st Grenadiers. If this were not enough, following the murder during the previous autumn by the IRA of the Gold Stick, Lord Mountbatten, another death was to come.

In November, 1982, the Silver Stick, Colonel Andrew Hartigan, had a fall on a road while hunting with the Grafton. He died of head injuries a week later in hospital, having never regained consciousness. 'Snip' Hartigan, who had commanded The Life Guards between 1976 and 1978, was both very popular and very able, the Regiment seeing all too little of him during numerous postings at Extra Regimental Employment. His death in part led to the vigorous and successful campaign to persuade those who ride horses, both military and

---

* His son later served in the Regiment for several years as a regular officer.

civilian, to wear hard hats. Colonel Andrew had been wearing the traditional silk top-hat when he fell.

Exercise 'Spearpoint 80' was the annual higher formation exercise at the end of the 1980 training season. However, A Squadron went back to Canada, on this occasion, with D Squadron, the Queen's Own Hussars, as part of the 1st Royal Welch Fusiliers' Battle Group. All of the squadrons were to go at some point during the tour, the regimental Battle Group going out in 1981.

The situation in Northern Ireland was relatively quiet, only averaging around eighty deaths through violence per year. The Regiment was only called on to provide one squadron (D, under Major James Ellery) as Guard Force for the Maze Prison in 1982. They there came under the command of 39 Infantry Brigade. This they promptly renamed 39 Guards Brigade as the commander was Brigadier Michael Hobbs of the Grenadiers and the brigade also contained the 2nd Coldstream Guards.

In January, 1981, Lieutenant Colonel James Emson assumed command, while Regimental Corporal Major John Leighton had taken over from his predecessor, now Lieutenant Andy Kelly of the Royal Armoured Corps Gunnery School, during the previous month. After twenty-two years of duty, either with the Regiment, at Knightsbridge or the Guards Depot, it was also time for Major Seymour Gilbart-Denham to move on, though in his case it was only as far as a staff appointment at Paderborn Garrison.

The winter was a good one for sports. Lieutenant Denis Darley, who had transferred from The Blues and Royals, proved a very able master and huntsman to the Weser Vale Hunt, while Major Nick D'Ambrumenil and Lieutenant Alastair Watson were, respectively, first and second in the Army Individual Cresta Run Championships at St. Moritz.

During the Summer the Regiment performed particularly well at the Rhine Army Summer Show, winning over £500 in prize money. Major Tony Goodhew MBE and the recently promoted Captain Darley, together with Lance Corporal of Horse Hague and Lance Corporal Burge being among the winners; and the polo team (Captains James Hewitt, Charlie Graham, Iain Forbes-Cockell and Darley) won both the BAOR Inter-Regimental and the Captains and Subalterns tournaments.

Standards were presented by Her Majesty The Queen to the Household Cavalry in 1983, with D Squadron (Major Tony Goodhew and Captain Iain Forbes-Cockell) representing the Regiment in a new generation of vehicles. Staff Corporal Lowry was largely responsible for converting the squadron's drivers to the Fox four-wheeled replacement for the Ferret, the Sultan and the Spartan both being tracked.

Later in the year Lieutenant Colonel Tim Earl assumed command, Captain Nick Holliday having become Adjutant and Chris Slater Regimental Corporal Major shortly before. The sabre squadron leaders now were Majors Peter Hunter, Hon. Nigel Adderley, Christopher Anderson (a former Gunner) and Tony Goodhew.

The Band came out before Christmas on their annual visit, Major Tony Richards, the Director of Music being dined out by the officers to mark his retirement after thirteen years with them. Captain Jerry McColl, from the Brigade of Gurkhas Band in Hong Kong, was to be the new Director. Mr Eric Lloyd performed the ceremony of 'Hanging the Brick', which was attended by fourteen Old Comrades whom Corporal of Horse Dean had brought out from England and in January, 1984, the Regiment came home to Windsor.

Chapter 13

Combermere: Armoured Reconnaissance (1975-1980, 1984-1989)

The Regiment, on their return to Combermere in October, 1975, were to find themselves deployed in much the same piecemeal fashion as had been the case during the late 'sixties under Lieutenant Colonel Desmond Langley. However before there was any deployment The Queen, accompanied by the Gold Stick, honoured the Regiment with a visit. After lunching with the officers, Her Majesty was shown around the barracks prior to meeting some of the soldiers and their wives.

Other visitors included the Major General (Philip Ward), Brigadier Peter Reid from 3rd Division and the Silver Stick, Colonel Jim Eyre, the latter pair being former Blues and Royals.

B Squadron were the first to leave. Under the command of Major Nick Lawson they left for a standard four-month emergency tour in Northern Ireland. Based at Aldergrove Airport, with troops scattered around the various RUC and Ulster Defence Regiment (UDR) posts, they acted as land-rover-borne infantry in an area of about 1,000 square miles. The tour was largely routine, the main event being an IRA mortar attack on the airport itself. This had an upsetting effect on the RAF personnel who had hitherto considered themselves immune from involvement in the troubles.

In February, 1976, Major Tim Earl and C Squadron, together with their Scorpion and Scimitar tracked vehicles and Volvo 'band wagons', back again in their role as part of the ACE mobile force, departed for Norway for training. The usual stories filtered back about 'the worst weather for twenty years' *et cetera*.

The next to leave (in March) for a now standard six-month tour with UNFICYP in Cyprus was Major John Bedells with A Squadron. As Force Reserve the squadron had a base in Nicosia and troops deployed and periodically rotated with the Danes, Austrians and Swedes. The Turks from the mainland had occupied the northern half of the island after their invasion two years previously and it was along the *de facto* border that A Squadron was required to spend much of their time in patrolling. Also the Turkish and Greek communities were still scrapping, so again it fell to the troops with their Ferrets to interpose themselves between the fighting factions, returning fire with the Browning if under direct attack themselves.

Lieutenant Peter Hunter had occasion to visit Famagusta, a large port on the eastern coast which hitherto had a predominantly Greek-Cypriot population: these 20,000 or so had all fled, leaving the Turkish-Cypriot minority in the old walled city, their usual abode. The rest, said Hunter, was like a ghost-town, with only the odd United Nations patrol.

2nd Lieutenant Simon Hayward became temporarily detached from two of his fingers (his driver and an Australian Policeman stuck them back on) after an incident with a mattock-wielding Turkish-Cypriot farmer; but the high point of the tour was perhaps the affair of the water. Lord Mountbatten had come out to visit the squadron at the end of May, and his itinerary included a trip to the troop post at Larnaca in the Austrian-controlled sector.

The lack of running water in the former seaside villa had been the object of numerous requests for action to Headquarters UNFICYP since the squadron's arrival in the island, without result. It was mentioned to the Gold Stick almost in conversation. However, Lord Mountbatten contacted the Force Commander, General Prem Chand, and told him that unless water flowed within the week, he would raise the matter with the United Nations' Secretary General, Kurt Waldheim. The water flowed thereafter.

Back at Windsor there was precious little left for Lieutenant Colonel Simon Cooper to command. In fact his allotted time was up and in August he handed over the Regiment to Lieutenant Colonel Andrew Hartigan, known to his friends as 'Snip' after expensive efforts to master the game of poker as a young officer in Egypt. Maurice Young also departed, in his case for civilian life; his place as Regimental Corporal Major was filled by Les Lumb, a very capable soldier (he eventually reached the rank of Lieutenant Colonel on the Staff) and a strict disciplinarian. The bane of his life at that time was Lieutenant David Naylor-Leyland's dog, Bear.

This Belgian Wolfhound had a penchant for goldfish, which could be found in the artificial pond outside the Warrant Officers' and Non-Commissioned Officers' mess, whither Bear would repair. There he would be arrested when the Regimental Corporal Major went on his rounds and locked in a cell until his owner could retrieve him.

1976 was also marked by a new commitment: security at London Airport. Terrorists of all persuasions were hijacking aircraft across the world almost at random, and it was decided that a show of force from time to time might act as a deterrent. To date the occasional presence of Household Cavalry armoured vehicles ('tanks' to the media), which are strictly in support of the civil police, appears to have worked.

Another commitment for the Regiment, towards the end of 1976, was Belize*, formerly British Honduras and now a Commonwealth member, which was feeling threatened by its larger neighbour, Guatemala. Accordingly Lieutenant David Bruton and a strengthened troop from C Squadron were the first to be sent out for a six-month tour to preserve *Pax Britannica* by reinforcing the existing garrison.

All of the squadrons carried out yet further tours in Ulster during 1977, which included B Squadron's tour of Dungannon during which no less than five soldiers were injured by gunshot. In addition C Squadron carried out their final exercise with the ACE mobile force, the requirement for the future being met by the RAC training regiment (at that time being the 17th/21st Lancers).

In April A Squadron under Major Clive Simpson Gee, a former Blue and Royal, went on an exchange with B Troop (a squadron equivalent) of the 1st Squadron of the 4th (US) Cavalry at Fort Riley, Texas, for six weeks. Lieutenant Peter Hunter recalled finding that the normal 'troop' consisted of three jeeps, three Sheridan tanks, two APC-mounted TOW missile launchers, an infantry section and a mortar vehicle.

What he found truly impressive was the integration at regimental level of the air troop. Unlike the British equivalent, where the Regiment's handful of unarmed Sioux helicopters in the late 'sixties described themselves as an 'Air Squadron', this troop, in addition to recce helicopters, contained nine Huey Cobra gunships. These could fire an assortment of weapons from the Gatling, with its cyclic rate of fire of 4,000 rounds per minute, to rockets and mortars. What he found less impressive was the American habit of centralized cooking in the field, after the British Cavalry habit of all vehicles being self-contained for rations and for cooking.

At the end of the tour the squadron dispersed all over the United States on five days' leave before flying back to England, where Captain Hunter became Adjutant in place of Captain Anthony De Ritter.

The winter of 1977/1978 was bedevilled by civil strikes. First there was the Bakers' Strike. This proved no problem within

---

* Captain James Astor later described his own six-month tour in Belize as being one of the most enjoyable periods of his service.

barracks: the bread that was made as a result in the cookhouse was so popular that there was a strong demand to continue with the practice after the strike was over.

Then came the Firemen's Strike. Not only did the firemen withdraw their labour, but they made it quite clear that they had no intention of allowing any 'black-leg' alternative force to use the fire-fighting engines and equipment, the property of the taxpayer. Back in the days of union appeasement the then socialist government were not prepared to challenge this, but they had one shot left in the locker: in the stocks of obsolescent Civil Defence equipment there existed a fleet of fire appliances of the 'Green Goddess' variety. These were made ready for the Army and the strike was eventually broken, but not before Life Guard firemen with one Green Goddess had been deployed fighting fires for several weeks, curiously under command of the Royal Navy in London District.

Lieutenant Colonel Arthur Gooch took command in 1978 and Regimental Corporal Major Andy Kelly took over from Les Lumb, who was commissioned. The Regiment were by then part of 6th Field Force, brigades having gone temporarily out of fashion. As such they went to northern Germany for the NATO exercise 'Bold Guard' and were, for perhaps the first time, under German command. Journeys by sea seemed always fraught with incident: in the previous year the LSL *Sir Lancelot* with A Squadron aboard, en route for exercise 'Lion Heart' had been so badly rammed by an Algerian tanker in Southampton Water that she was forced to put back into Marchwood military port. A Squadron's participation in the exercise had to be cancelled.

1980 was a fairly quiet year to start with, apart from the Ambulance Drivers' Strike in which the Regiment were far more heavily committed than they had been with the Firemen's Strike. The Regiment drew up forty army ambulances in January which were then deployed at police stations in the London area. Escorted by police patrol cars they were responsible for collecting casualties (with the help of RAMC personnel − later Musicians from the Band) and taking them to hospital. Captain Derek Stratford acted as control at New Scotland Yard.

A Squadron were the first to start conversion to the Chieftain prior to the return to Detmold after the turn of the year; B Squadron completed a six-month tour in Cyprus; while C Squadron, bereft of the ACE mobile force role, remained operational with 6th Field Force.

To the delight of the Gold Stick, himself often described as the father of modern polo, the Regiment won both the 1979 Inter-Regimental and the Captains' and Subalterns' polo tournaments. He attended the final of the latter and presented the cup to the Regimental team (Captain Peter Hunter, Lieutenant Iain Forbes-Cockell, 2nd Lieutenants Charlie Graham and James Hewitt) after their six goals to three win over the Royal Navy team. 'Colonel Dickie' went on holiday to Ireland, as was his custom, during the following week. It was there, on 27 August, that he was murdered by the IRA, who had placed a bomb in the small boat that he used for entertaining members of his family.

Admiral of the Fleet Earl Mountbatten of Burma KG, GCB, OM, GCSI, GCIE, GCVO, DSO had been a good Colonel to The Life Guards. Although talking to members of the 'lower deck' did not, perhaps, come naturally to one who had held plenipotentiary powers as the last Viceroy of India, he appeared to realize this. He made great efforts to visit the regiment, or squadrons, wherever they happened to be and to talk to all ranks. Members of both the regiment and the regimental Association who later took part in his funeral at Westminster Abbey, did so with great pride at having been associated with such a fine man.

On 22 October, 1979, The Queen was pleased to appoint Major General Lord Michael Fitzalan Howard KCVO, CB, CBE, MC as Gold Stick in Waiting and as Colonel, The Life Guards. Colonel Michael, a former Scots Guard and Major General from 1969 to 1971, was then Marshal of the Diplomatic Corps and physically not dissimilar to Field Marshal Sir Gerald Templer, Colonel of The Blues and Royals.

Finally, after a farewell visit from The Queen in November, in February,1980, Lieutenant Colonel Arthur Gooch took the Regiment back to Detmold and Chieftain tanks.

Four years later, in January, 1984, Lieutenant Colonel Tim Earl with his Adjutant Captain David Waterhouse and Regimental Corporal Major Chris Slater brought them back to Combermere for what might be The Life Guards' last tour there as a full regiment. By now brigades were back in vogue and they found themselves as part of the 5th Airborne Brigade, based at nearby Aldershot.

If previous generations of Life Guards had regarded those who left aircraft other than by ramp or steps as being mentally deranged, Colonel James Emson excepted, and the Royal Air Force as a rather dubious air-line used for taking soldiers abroad and back, then this was the watershed. By the time that Lieutenant Colonel James Ellery took the Regiment to Sennelager five years later, some thirty soldiers (and a dozen officers including himself) were parachute trained. This was to enable the brigade to insert a troop or more of Scorpion CVRs and a tactical headquarters by airdrop.

However the first deployment was due to be the despatch of A Squadron to Beirut. Lebanon was to collapse into full civil war the following year, but in the meanwhile a multi-national peace-keeping force was trying, vainly, to hold the ring. This had resulted, two years earlier, in the deaths of 241 American marines and fifty-seven French paratroopers caused by suicide bombers; in the logic of the Middle East this was in retaliation for the massacre of Palestinian refugees in the Sabra and Chatila camps by Israeli-condoned militia.

The 16th/5th Lancers had a squadron out there, and it was to them that Major Peter Hunter and Captain (QM) Bruce Payne went on a four-day reconnaissance. On a visit to the French-held heliport down at the harbour, which was attracting a certain amount of incoming sniper fire, they saw an RAF Chinook helicopter fly in and lower its ramp, the twin rotors still turning for a quick get-away. Down the ramp strode the familiar figure of Major General Sir Desmond Langley, currently commanding British Forces, Cyprus. Oblivious of being under fire, he proceeded to 'sharpen up' two French sentries who were cowering in their sangars. Major Hunter whisked him away to the British base before he could provoke the French into some disastrous reaction!

Shortly after their return to Combermere Prime Minister Margaret Thatcher, sensing the mayhem that seemed inevitable, recalled the 16th/5th and stood down A Squadron.

C Squadron (Major Stewart Vetch) in the meanwhile were off for a standard tour in Cyprus and the assault troops of A and B Squadrons headed in the other direction, to Belize. The remainder were soon off to Germany on Exercise Lionheart '84 which on this occasion was billed as the largest mobilization and deployment of British troops since the Second World War. The Regiment (Major Peter Hunter's A Squadron with CVR(T)s and Major Hon. Nigel Adderley's B Squadron with CVR(W) Foxes) and the remainder of the brigade joined up with the Americans, Dutch and Germans to provide a credible enemy for 1st (British) Corps.

The Regiment acquitted themselves well. The exercise was enlivened by Lieutenant James Hoare's capture of the Duke of Westminster, serving at the time with the Cheshire Yeomanry (TA). 'Go for his wallet, not his maps!' Hoare, a reservist, was ordered by the brigadier. An officer in the 13th/18th Hussars was apparently arrested and jailed (temporarily one hopes) for capturing a German general found behind the lines before the manoeuvres had even started*. And the Regiment's last stand was at a village with the unlikely name of Unterpantshausen.

Two changes had resulted from the Regiment's adoption of the new range of CVRs, and latterly coming under command of airborne forces. The first was that the A (fighting) vehicles tended to be moved for any distance on land by containers, or even furniture-type vans; this saved track-mileage.

The second was what had previously been referred to loosely as 'Airportability'. When practised, this involved RAF aircrew anchoring the vehicles to the floor of the aircraft with sufficient restraints to withstand up to twenty times the force of gravity. Now the essence was on speed: the vehicles were expected to be driving down the ramp and in action within seconds of touch-down.

This last was in practice for exercise Purple Victory in the autumn of 1985: elements of the Regiment, together with the brigade, flew to Northumberland, regarded for the duration as a different country despite Geordie pleas to the contrary.

The autumn was also the time for another change at the top: Lieutenant Colonel Tony Goodhew MBE assumed command, with Ian Kelly as his Regimental Corporal Major. Major James Ellery was the Second in Command and Captain Charlie Graham became Adjutant following the turn of the year

1986 was par for the course for a regiment at Windsor: B Squadron (Major John Bayley) went to Cyprus, C Squadron (Major Iain Forbes-Cockell) to Texas, and A Squadron (Major Anthony De Ritter) went to Norway with the 3rd Royal Marine Commando Brigade. Matters were rather more exciting on the sporting front, however. The rugby team won, for the first time, the Prince of Wales's Cup, while the shooting team won both of the RAC competitions at Bisley**; the Captains and Subalterns polo team won their tournament for the third year in succession; Captain John Sunnucks was beaten by a short head in the Grand Military; Lieutenant Dominic Mahony qualified for a place in both the national fencing and pentathlon teams; and Corporal of Horse Margan's fencing team won a Silver Medal at the Commonwealth Games.

---

* It later transpired that the officer, the local landowner, was driving back to his castle for a bath. He took a poor view of being searched, Northern Ireland-style, in front of his villagers.

** Much of the successes at Bisley and elsewhere were due to the enthusiasm and determination in the 'eighties of Captain (QM) Les Lumb.

Major James Ellery took sixteen Life Guards for a three-week course with P (for Pegasus) Company at the Parachute Depot. 'There is nothing terribly difficult about P Company,' he wrote afterwards, having been one of the four who passed, which was about par for the course. He was being too modest, as those who may have either been on the course themselves, or saw the Channel Four programme on the Company in 1992, may bear witness. Ellery's aim was to have at least one troop per squadron fully parachute-trained, but in the event only one troop in the Regiment was ready in the time available.

If the Army had learned the hard way over Suez in 1956 that the days of the troopship were numbered, so it learned in the Falkland Islands' campaign of 1982 the importance of physical fitness. The days of protracted lunches in all of the messes were over; it was the time of the lean and hungry look and Corporal Majors were to be seen going for runs at lunchtime. The joker in the pack at this time was one Trooper Nutt, an outstandingly fit man who also smoked like the proverbial chimney. He used to infuriate the instructors at P Company by asking for permission to go for a run every evening when both students and instructors were exhausted!

It was also the time for the final retirement of Lieutenant Colonel (Staff QM) Dennis Meakin after forty-five years of service. After enlisting in 1941 he had been squadron clerk to Sir Arthur Collins and Chief Clerk to Sir Henry Abel Smith (both Blues) with the 2nd Household Cavalry Regiment. Superintending Clerk at Horse Guards followed before periods as Quartermaster to both the Regiment and the mounted regiment. His service had ended as Assistant Regimental Adjutant at Headquarters, Household Cavalry, as a Retired Officer (RO), and Curator of the Household Cavalry Museum. He remains (1992) as secretary of the Officers' Dining Club.

1987 was another routine year, except for B Squadron. Under Local Lieutenant Colonel Simon Falkner they were in charge of Earl's Court for the period of the Royal Tournament. This sadly interfered with the squadron leader's sailing plans!

Lieutenant Dominic Mahony's team won a bronze medal in the World Pentathlon Championships, as indeed they were to in the 1988 Seoul Olympics: Corporal of Horse Margan remained listed for the Games. The polo team's regulars also received a boost of new talent in the form of Captains Hon. Milo Watson and Christopher Mitford-Slade, and 2nd Lieutenant Rupert MacKenzie-Hill.

Lieutenant Colonel James Ellery assumed command in June, 1988, with Captain and Adjutant Christopher Mitford-Slade and Regimental Corporal Major Tony Mead as his team at Regimental Headquarters.

After being right-hand man to his predecessor, thus largely responsible for training, Ellery was now able to consolidate the considerable gains that were to lead to acceptance as an equal partner by the Airborne Brigade.

One not altogether welcome, but necessary, result of this streamlined role was the slimming down of the amount of personal kit that an individual could take with him on exercise. The current range of CVRs did not allow for the *impedimenta* that could be carried on the Chieftain, nor even on the Saladin. An individual carried only what he could fit into his Bergen pack.

From the airborne forces' reluctance to deploy the two CVR(T) sabre troops* of The Blues and Royals that were present in the Falklands six years earlier, the parachute battalions within the brigade were now demanding the light armoured support that the Regiment was able to provide. Following the success of the Israeli raid on Entebbe, Uganda, where special forces rescued the kidnapped passengers of an El Al aircraft, came the Tactically Air Landed Operations (TALO) for the British Airborne. The drill, honed to a fine degree, was for up to four Hercules C-130 transport aircraft to be flown under radar cover to the destination, land simultaneously, off-load a sabre troop or more of CVR(T)s and a company of men and to be in the air again within forty-five seconds.

When this was first demonstrated with the SAS to the Ministry of Defence, whose observers were seated on the target, the latter were unaware of anything taking place before the Scorpions opened fire with their main (76mm) armament.

The final role that the Regiment were called upon to carry out was acting as escorts to the American Cruise inter-continental ballistic missiles and their launch vehicles, which were based at Greenham Common, near Newbury. These vehicles would practise deployment, normally in the Salisbury Plain area, from time to time and would require escorting to and from their base, if for no other reason than to protect their crews from the fanatical women who were encamped outside the gates of the base. These harridans stalked them wherever they went, intent on causing damage and embarrassment to American and British servicemen alike.

The Regiment took part in no less than five exercises with the 5th Airborne Brigade during 1989 during which Regimental Headquarters and a Scorpion troop were air-dropped (as opposed to air-landed) on each occasion in advance of the air-landed remainder of the Regiment.

* A CVR(T) Sabre Troop consisted of two Scorpions and two Scimitar tracked vehicles.

127

Shortly before Christmas The Queen inspected the Airborne Troop on Smith's Lawn, Windsor Great Park, (more usually home to the Guards' Polo Club) before being driven to Combermere, with a CVR(T) escort, to visit the whole Regiment.

1989 was also the year in which the Berlin Wall came down.

Chapter 14

Iraq (1990-1991)

The Life Guards moved back to Germany, this time to Athlone Barracks, Sennelager, and to a new tank, the Challenger, in January, 1990. Lieutenant Colonel James Ellery, who had eleven months of his appointment yet to run, now had Captain Hugh Robertson as his Adjutant and John Belza as Regimental Corporal Major, while Major Christopher Anderson was the Second in Command.

The Blues and Royals had moved to Sennelager from Detmold two years earlier, taking the black horse troop and the Weser Vale Bloodhounds with them. The horses were now stabled in the grandly titled Rhine Army (Sennelager) Equestrian Centre and were controlled by Captain (LE) Sandy Sanderson, whose wife, Jane, whipped-in to the hounds together with 2nd Lieutenant James Gaselee. (The pack was hunted by Captain Tom Thorneycroft, a joint-master together with Majors James Hewitt and Christopher Anderson.)

As a result of the equestrian infrastructure, the Regiment had a great deal of success in the summer shows and hunter trials: Major Anderson, Captain Dominic Mahony, Captains (QM) Chris Slater and Ian Kelly, Corporal of Horse Maxwell and Lance Corporal of Horse Peers being among the leading regimental competitors.

Although the Berlin Wall was down, the Warsaw Pact about to disintegrate and the communist leaders of the East Europe countries falling one by one, the Commanding Officer saw no reason to relax the high standards of readiness achieved in the 5th Airborne Brigade. Indeed his directive, issued on arrival to squadron leaders and down to Corporal Majors, left the readers in no doubt as to his attitude to operational preparedness on the one hand and on the other to the treatment liable to be meted out to those who were found using drugs, or alcohol to excess.

Conversion training was completed by April,1990, so the Regiment went to Soltau for troop training, where a change awaited them. Germany was now in the throes of a 'green' revolution which in turn seemed to mean that what had, since the Second World War, been a strictly military training area, had now to be shared with picnickers, motor-cyclists, bird-watchers and the like. And woe betide any soldier who was careless enough to spill a drop of fuel or oil when replenishing his vehicle!

A Squadron (Major James Hewitt) found themselves attached to the 3rd Light Infantry, while the remainder of the Regiment formed a battle group, together with two companies of the Light Infantry, as part of the 33rd Armoured Brigade, and were due to go to Canada for training later in the year. It therefore fell to A Squadron, being detached, to provide the (nuclear) site guards and later to lay on, with the 3rd Royal Fusiliers, a demonstration for General Snetkov, the Soviet Commander of Western Group Forces, Germany. 2nd Lieutenant Giles Howson, one of the three Russian speakers in the Regiment, was able to introduce the General to his crew.

Then on 2 August, 1990, Iraq invaded Kuwait* over an oil dispute and seemed to threaten Saudi Arabia and her enormous oilfields. All three countries had been within the British sphere of influence at some point since the Second World War and all three contained a large number of expatriate British businessmen and their families. The United States sent 4,000 troops from their 82nd Airborne and F-15 fighter aircraft to Saudi Arabia within the week, to be followed during September by a brigade from both the British (code-name Operation Granby) and the French. Most of the major powers sent naval craft to the Gulf, recently cleared of mines left by the Iranians during their eight-year inconclusive war with Iraq.

Any hopes that the Regiment might be sent were quickly dashed; 7th Armoured was the brigade warned. Moreover, the Regiment had to hand over their new Challenger Mark III tanks to the Royal Scots Dragoon Guards. They, together with the Queen's Royal Irish Hussars, were bound for the Gulf. The Life Guards battle group, including B and C Squadrons, therefore departed for Canada as planned. Hardly had they left than the decision was taken to send another brigade (4th Armoured) to the Gulf, so A Squadron were required to hand over their second issue of tanks to the 14th/20th Hussars. That done, on 27 November the squadron were told by the Commanding Officer that they were to provide a fourth sabre squadron for that regiment, to be entitled 'The Life Guards Squadron, 14th/20th King's Hussars'. And so yet another fleet of Challenger tanks had to be prepared!

Most of the early part of December was taken up with both day and night firing at Hohne and in getting to know their 'new' regiment which was commanded by Lieutenant Colonel Mike

* Iraq had threatened to do this in both 1959 and 1961.

Vickery. They were made up to a strength of 120 all ranks, which included Captain Rupert MacKenzie-Hill, recently back from the Pathfinder Platoon with 5th Airborne Brigade, as battle captain. On Boxing Day they left for the Gulf where the squadron leader, Major James Hewitt, was spotted days later on television sunbathing in the desert sand in front of Prime Minister John Major!

It was at this time that the commanding officers changed: Lieutenant Colonel James Ellery, whose single-mindedness in training the Regiment had brought them to a peak, had the mortification of seeing them go to war without him. Lieutenant Colonel Anthony De Ritter took command.

The remainder of the Regiment in the meanwhile had been warned for deployment in the theatre as Battlefield Casualty Replacements, so they spent a week in the Sennelager Training Centre in early January honing their individual skills before departure.

Pressure on Iraq's President Saddam Hussein through the United Nations and through individual peace initiatives had by this stage almost run out. The American Secretary of State, James Baker, had in the meanwhile put together a coalition of thirty wildly disparate nations to oppose Iraq, at the same time ensuring that Israel, Iran and the Soviet bloc stayed neutral.

Since King Fahd of Saudi Arabia is also 'Guardian of the Holy Places' to the Muslim World, considerable efforts were made to ensure that such places were not to be defiled by the habits of the largely Christian Coalition army. Alcohol was banned throughout, much to the delight of those responsible for discipline; and Padres, always in plentiful supply when action is imminent, had to be described as 'Welfare Officers' during much of the campaign.

By 15 January, 1991, General Norman Schwarzkopf, Commander US Forces, had over one third of a million ground forces, including 25,000 British, under command; while Lieutenant General Prince Khaled bin Sultan, the Saudi Commander, had just under 100,000 which included French, Syrian and Egyptian ground forces. Estimates varied wildly over the enemy strengths, but they were known to be dug in in depth north of the Kuwait - Saudi border with a biological and chemical capability.

It is unlikely that Schwarzkopf was aware of it, but one of his command was unique: for Surgeon Captain Charles Goodson-Wickes MP, a Life Guard reservist, was the only member of the House of Commons to rejoin the colours for the duration of hostilities. Promoted to Surgeon Lieutenant Colonel by Simon Cooper, the Major General, before departure, he was greeted with 'I was a Lance

Corporal when we last met, Colonel!' by Squadron Corporal Major David Evans when he briefly looked in on A Squadron.

After helping to establish a tented British Field Hospital behind the left flank (they were warned to expect up to eight per cent casualties when the ground war started) he wangled himself a post as Medical Officer to Brigadier Patrick Cordingley's 7th Armoured Brigade Headquarters with whom he later swept into Iraq.

On 16 January, 1991, the Air War started and air supremacy was established very soon, a large part of the enemy aircraft fleeing to Iran where they were impounded. On 24 February the ground war, which was to last for 100 hours, started with Coalition forces entering Iraq.

2nd Lieutenant David London commanded 4 Troop in A Squadron which was part of the 14th/20th Hussars in the 4th Armoured Brigade. He wrote this account on his return to Germany.

On 26 December, 1990, the advance party of A Squadron, The Life Guards, commanded by Major James Hewitt, left Hanover Airport for Dhahran in Saudi Arabia. The preceding two months had been the most frustrating imaginable for the squadron. Twice we had brought tanks up to the peak of maintenance and performance; twice we were obliged to watch them go to the Gulf in other hands. B and C Squadrons, meanwhile, were exercising on the British army training area in Suffield,Canada: perhaps it is not surprising that we sometimes felt left out of the action. It seemed that we only had the possibility of participation to look forward to, if indeed the crisis could be made to last long enough for us to make an appearance.

Then came the news that we were to take on the style and title of The Life Guards Squadron, 14th/20th King's Hussars. We first met our adoptive Commanding Officer, Lieutenant Colonel Mike Vickery, at Hohne, as we fired yet another clutch of tanks that were not to be our own, and where we were hailed as the best squadron to fire on the Operation Granby range programme.

There followed a short but intensive period of fitness, NBC, recognition and signals training at Athlone Barracks, and a brief stay with the 14th/20th at Munster for 'Familiarisation and Documentation' and further training. Seldom have NBC and recognition instructors enjoyed such undivided attention from their classes! Our projected departure dates did not allow for Christmas in England, so we sped home for a hasty week's leave, returning on Christmas Eve to spend the festive season in what, for the next three months, was to be the bosom of our family.

At 0100 hours local time on 30 December, 1990, the main body touched down at Al Jubail Military Airport in Saudi Arabia, and made its way to Blackadder Camp, which at that time was barely a shadow of the vast accommodation centre it was to become. Introduced the same day to their fourth tanks in three months, the crews got down to what, by that stage, they knew best, and soon had the vehicles in operational state, ready to move into the desert on New Year's Day. We would then have less than two weeks to assimilate how to move about this unfamiliar lunar landscape, both tactically and in terms of simple day and night navigation, before we were expected to be ready to take part in battle-group and subsequently brigade exercises.

The UN deadline set for 15 January came and went with no apparent impact on our training programme, although the start of the air war two days later and the almost immediate Scud* attack on Israel were of course the subject of much discussion and speculation. The latter event threw a pall of gloom over the whole squadron. There followed a five-week period during which we expected at any moment to be detailed for action, but which in fact saw only continued air bombardment of the Iraqi forces and cities, and sporadic Scud attacks on Israel, Riyadh and Al Jubail. It was a source of ironic amusement to us that we, deployed in the desert, were in fact less inconvenienced by the war than those at Blackadder Camp on whom we heaped such scorn, but who, we learned, were turned out of their beds twice or three times nightly to take cover in trenches and bunkers.

On 19 January we sustained our first and fortunately only serious casualty. 2nd Lieutenant Johnny Wheeler, troop leader of 3 Troop, had his foot crushed in the traverse of his tank and was evacuated to England. He was replaced by 2nd Lieutenant Pip Earl of C Squadron who, with the rest of the Regiment, was by now in theatre as part of the Battle Casualty Replacement chain. These BCR Life Guards were ultimately equipped with War Maintenance Reserve tanks, and, had the action lasted longer, would probably have been committed to

---

* The thirty-year-old Scud B has been accurately described as 'little more than a gas tanker with a grenade on the end'. Of Soviet and North Korean origin, with modifications the ground-launched missiles had a range of up to 500 miles. Thus Riyadh, Dhahran and Jerusalem were all within range. Most of those that were fired from mobile launchers during the campaign were intercepted by the American ground-to-air Patriot anti-missile missiles.

action also. In fact, B Squadron had the frustrating experience of entering Iraq on tank transporters, while C Squadron were not able to get out of Saudi Arabia before the cessation of hostilities.

On exercise and on transporter we gradually crept northwards and westwards towards the Wadi Al Batin and the tri-national border area. Then, on 22 February, James Hewitt returned from the battle-group commander's orders group with orders for our move through the Iraqi defences and into Iraq itself. We were to move out two days later. Better still, the Troop Leaders were able to mark on their maps the very positions which had been earmarked for our personal attention; in the words of Brigadier Christopher Hammerbeck, 4 Brigade Commander, it was 'just the sort of target to cut your teeth on. A company of T55s [tanks] and two companies of mechanized infantry. All facing in the wrong direction!'

Clad in full NBC suits against the expected chemical attacks which never came, and with our vehicles adorned with luminous panels to assist our aircraft in recognizing us, the Royal Scots battle-group, commanded by Lieutenant Colonel Iain Johnstone and led by The Life Guards Squadron, entered Iraq at 1415 hours on 25 February, arriving at our forming-up point at 1800 hours. There was no moon, no stars, and a persistent cold drizzle was falling. In these murky conditions the Multi Launch Rocket System (MLRS) artillery made a brilliant fireworks display as it pounded the enemy positions prior to our arrival. A new objective consisting of twenty M46 guns was identified and allocated to us.

At 1930 hours the battle-group moved out and five kilometres from the objective shook out into assault formation. Every 1,000 metres James Hewitt updated the Squadron on the range to the first identified enemy locations, until at 1,000 metres 3 Troop reported the first contact, and the Squadron began engaging targets. The enemy, thrown into confusion by the arrival in their rear of the tanks which filled the air with their screaming engine-note, not to mention 120mm main armament and machine-gun fire, surrendered in their hundreds. Continuing to sweep forwards, The Life Guards had little time to deal with prisoners, and vehicle commanders could only gesture to them to wait for the arrival of The Royal Scots, coming up close behind.

The Squadron was then ordered to proceed to its original

objective. The plan was to attack from north to south, dividing the enemy positions into three 'bite-sized pieces', to use the Divisional Commander's phrase. We were to reorganize on a tarred road, to the South of which the 14th/20th Hussars were performing a similar task. As before, the enemy were surprised by the direction and sheer violence of our attack, and had no time to respond. The Squadron destroyed five tanks, several armoured personnel carriers, and various guns and mortars. Once again, numerous prisoners were taken and dealt with by the Battle Captain, Rupert MacKenzie-Hill, before being passed rearwards via The Royal Scots to the prisoner of war handling force. The Squadron ambulance treated several Iraqi wounded, some of whom could barely be restrained in their eagerness to show their gratitude.

The battle-group now went firm to await replenishment of fuel and ammunition. It was now midday on 26 February. In the evening James Hewitt attended Colonel Iain's Orders Group and was tasked with a further multiple objective, consisting of a regiment of artillery, a company of tanks and two companies of infantry. We crossed the start line at 0030 hours and immediately had to defile over a half-sunken pipeline, thus presenting our most vulnerable aspect to the enemy — the underbelly of our tanks. Amid reports of sightings of T72s [tanks] and armoured personnel carriers, suggesting the presence of the Republican Guard Force, we assaulted the first objective. Scanning the area with our Thermal Observation Gunnery Sights, we identified a large amount of equipment, but no movement of vehicles or men.

Searching coaxial machine-gun fire elicited no response, so after immobilizing any fighting vehicles the Battlegroup moved on to the second position. Here again there were many vehicles but the area seemed to be deserted. This time, however, our searching fire flushed out two groups of surrendering Iraqis, who were quickly picked up by the foremost Warriors (armoured personnel carriers) of The Royal Scots, who were becoming particularly adept at this kind of task. We rolled on towards the third objective, driving through a belt of anti-personnel mines which exploded under our tracks, blowing off the track pads; once more we found little sign of life. We later learned from prisoners that many of the Iraqis in that area had deserted when the Allied advance began two days earlier. We ended the attack shortly before dawn on 27 February, and were at once directed north to form a welcoming committee for a force of T72s which were reported to be moving fifteen miles to our front.

By mid-afternoon the enemy had still not appeared and we were instructed to move east across the Kuwaiti border, and to make best speed to a position to the north-west of Kuwait City. From there we would engage the Iraqi forces in retreat. In the confusion of this hasty move, and in the fading daylight, the 14th/20th Hussars battle-group inadvertently engaged two Spartan vehicles of the Royal Artillery and the advance was halted for the night. For many of us it was our first opportunity to sleep since 0600 hours on 25 February.

At 0630 on the morning of 28 February we continued the move towards Kuwait City. As daylight increased, large groups of Iraqi soldiers gravitated towards the battle-group in an attempt to surrender, but we had no time to deal with them. At 0800 hours it was announced that hostilities had been suspended; we were ordered to halt there in the desert twenty-five miles from Kuwait City. We remained at that very spot for a further two weeks before being regrouped with the 14th/20th Hussars and flying back to a cold and rainy Germany on 1 April.

Our job as part of the International Force in the Middle East was to restore the *status quo ante* in Kuwait by driving out the Iraqi aggressor. We are proud to have had the distinction of contributing to the speedy and successful execution of that task, and to have done so without loss of life to any Life Guard. We have pride in having done what was asked of us to the best of our ability, and to have brought credit to the Regiment.

Major James Hewitt, A Squadron Leader, was Mentioned in Despatches in the subsequent Gulf Honours List, an honour that reflected not only on his leadership, but also on the professionalism and efficiency of his squadron.

Writing from the comfort of home and with the gift of hindsight, it was inconceivable that the professional and predominantly American Coalition forces would not prevail against a third-world conscript army equipped with obsolescent weapons. With the spectre of Vietnam ever present for the Americans, they could afford neither to lose, nor to sustain unacceptable casualties in any Pyrrhic victory.

The American Deputy Defence Secretary, Lawrence Eagleburger, stated afterwards that Saddam Hussein had been threatened with 'extreme retaliation' (he declined to be more specific) had biological or chemical agents been used by Iraq. But the men on the ground, though all NBC trained and inoculated, did not know what to expect as they entered the battle area.

Major Giles Stibbe commanded C Squadron, The Life Guards. His account is as follows:

Wednesday morning, 16 January, 1991, B and C Squadrons, led respectively by Major David Waterhouse and me, reported to Sennelager Movement Control Check Point (MCCP). Eventually in the late afternoon we went by coach and four-ton truck to Hanover. There we met up with other passengers: mostly Queen's Own Highlanders en route to guard 1st Armoured Division Headquarters. There was a flight delay, so we were taken to a nearby RAMC barracks for a 'tea meal', then back to the airport and a last legal drink of alcohol before embarking on an RAF Tristar. Waterhouse was feeling bad effects from the vaccinations! Take-off and last glimpse of civilised European lights!

About 0100 hrs 17 January the tannoy announced: 'We're turning back. It's Started!' It turned out that the Identity Friend or Foe Kit (IFF), which had caused the initial flight delay from Hanover, wasn't working. So we turned back over Yugoslavia to Brize Norton. We managed to catch snippets of President Bush's declaration of war over the World Service until we landed when we watched Breakfast TV. We were told we would wait for forty-eight hours. This shortened to sixteen hours! Our flight approach to Al Jubayl was low level over the sand dunes, all too reminiscent of Oman where I had spent two years on Loan Service.

As we approached the airfield, the vast extent of the US war effort became obvious: from horizon to horizon were tanks, APCs, trucks, jeeps, helicopters and transport aircraft. We had been told to put on our NBC suits before landing and adopt the crash position: a sensible if melodramatic RAF precaution. When the aircraft door finally opened the waft of desert air brought memories of Oman rushing back!

We eventually retrieved our packs and began to stagger under their weight across the sand as night quickly fell and waited for 'clapped-out' Saudi buses driven by drivers whose main understandable concern was to barter for gas masks! They drove us through a no black-out downtown Al Jubayl to the docks which were defended by batteries of Patriot missiles. In a huge

137

customs shed we were fed and booked into the war zone. Then back onto the coaches with our kit to Blackadder Camp.

There, in the proverbial small hours, we were greeted by a Drill Sgt from 1st Scots Guards who briefed us and showed us to our 160lb tents after another welcome meal. Before turning-in we dug trenches. This was quite a novel experience for the commanders! The lowest rank present was a Lance Corporal of Horse! Eventually, knackered, we managed to flop onto camp beds or sleeping mats. Sleeping bags were too hot especially if one wore NBC kit. Then began what was to be an all too familiar nocturnal routine. We realized a few days later that the Americans sounded their sirens as soon as they detected a SCUD take off from Iraq. The British waited until they identified roughly where the SCUD was heading. To no avail as we were surrounded by Yanks! The first night we were in and out of trenches, and eventually fell asleep huddled together with our gas masks on!

When day broke it was reassuring to find the Scots Guards firmly in command and sharpening up a tented camp that must have resembled the worst aspects of MASH* until they arrived and got a grip. A daily routine of fitness training, small arms ranges, briefs, sangar building and general preparation started until the main Life Guard party arrived led by the Commanding Officer and Regimental Headquarters troop who took up command post Battle Casualty Replacement slots. The Scots Guards were exemplary hosts. This was to prove useful subsequently when we all met up in the Armoured Delivery Group and developed desert tactics without European confines!

The Scots Guards Captain (QM) Ron Cleminson had been David Waterhouse's Brigade Squad Instructor fifteen years earlier. So a tremendous rapport developed, and he did invaluable work extricating kit like desert combat uniforms from the logistic chaos that was prevalent in Al Jubayl port. The chaos occurred because container after container would arrive, yet there were not enough logisticians to check their contents. We eventually replaced our jungle green lightweight suits three weeks after arrival; tanks were just about ready to move when the land campaign started, but until then spares were as rare as could be!

As we waited to move up to join our tanks we spent several

* A popular television comedy about an American Field Hospital in the Korean War.

138

days talking tactics and practising basic drills such as NBC and First Aid that are usually only concentrated on at Troop Test time! The weather throughout the campaign was like a hot English summer with occasional spectacular storms.

At the end of January B and C Squadrons were moved, carrying everything we could by bus, Hercules transport planes, and eight-ton trucks up country to the Force Forward Maintenance Area (FFMA). Here we encountered the splendid Armoured Delivery Squadron which, under command of a redoubtable Royal Tank Regiment Major (now Lieutenant Colonel) (QM) Brian Broadhurst, had done a remarkable job during the previous four months trying to repair, and in some cases almost rebuild, the dregs of the British tank and armoured car fleet. Broadhurst had two teams: one from the Royal Tank Regiment and one from the 9th/12th Lancers who were worth their weight in platinum and were responsible for 'Heavy Metal' and armoured cars respectively.

It was reassuring to watch our two squadrons and recce troop, three troops from the Royal Hussars and two crews, one each from the 4th Royal Tank Regiment and the 4th/7th Dragoon Guards, get stuck into preparing their vehicles. Away from the inevitable bullshit of daily barrack routine a terrific camaraderie developed. All tanks were up-armoured on their sides and fronts and most had armoured charge bins fitted: a painstaking task.

On Saint Valentine's Day (February 14), Major Waterhouse and I were helicoptered with the Scots Guards company commanders up to 7th Armoured Brigade Headquarters. There we had an inspirational brief from Brigadier Patrick Cordingley and useful chats with Scots Dragoon Guards and Queen's Royal Irish Hussars counterparts. We were also told The Plan which seemed impressively daring. On our return the Armoured Delivery Group (ADG) began to shape up. In command was Lieutenant Colonel Seymour Monro of 1st Queen's Own Highlanders. His own troops were guarding formation headquarters as far apart as Riyadh and 1st Armoured Division (Main)! Monro commanded close reconnaissance troop and our two squadrons, which became three when D Squadron, The Life Guards, was resurrected under command of the Operations Officer, Captain Nick Garrett; a medium recce squadron of 9th/12th Lancers under Maj Harry Robertson; and three companies of Scots Guards under Majors Jan de Halvegang, Mark Turner, and Rory Ingleby-Mackenzie. There were also a few gunners and some armoured engineers. The whole force was supported by Headquarter Company, 1st Queen's Own Highlanders.

The Squadron/Company battle-groups had two useful days practising drills and tactics. The speed, protection and firepower of Challenger tanks was complemented by that of the Scots Guards' Warrior armoured personnel carriers, and the desert proved ideal for practising the momentum of shock action bounding one objective after another. The tank squadrons had a useful day's firing on an American range, and we then 'bombed up' with the titanium-tipped fin-stabilized armour-piercing rounds.

On 18 February Colonel Seymour gave an awe-inspiring 'O' Group. Here he confirmed The Plan, told us we could fully brief our troops, and then went on to describe the Armoured Delivery 'Modus Operandi'. Due to the shortage of tank transporters the ADG was to be divided in half. Each half was commanded either by Main or Step-Up Headquarters of the Highlanders. We practised this deployment on our final transporter move forward to the Divisional Assembly Area. This was north-west of Hafir al Batin on the wadi that runs north-east into Kuwait from Saudi. This wadi was the boundary between the Arab alliance forces and the US Army, French and British contingents.

Events then began to move fast. The ADG received its final visits from our Commanding Officer and that of the Scots Guards, both of whom must have been very frustrated not to command their own troops. Colonel Anthony reported that A Squadron were grouped as spearhead of the Royal Scots battle group. We were waiting for the final three-day ultimatum to run out, when on Day Two Colonel Seymour summoned his 'O' group to tell us that, due to the atrocities reported from Kuwait City, we were on six hours' notice to Move! There followed really impressive artillery barrages. B Squadron set off with the first half of the ADG group; the remainder of us waited, listening to the World Service, BFBS, and the American Forces 198 service! On the afternoon of D+1 we managed to radio through to Captain Tom Thorneycroft who was attached to 4th Armoured Brigade Headquarters. He told us he was guarding an Iraqi general!

The most frightening moment of the whole campaign for me occurred the next night a few days after we had watched Patriots shoot down Scuds over the local Saudi town, Hafir al Batin. The night sky was usually so clear that we watched fighters escorting bombers which were refuelling overhead before they continued their missions into Iraq. They looked like psychedelic shooting stars against the white of the Milky Way.

The days 24 to 28 February were stormy. In the middle of one night there were several loud explosions. These sounded to me as I quickly gained consciousness like a fusillade of SCUDS landing very close by, thoughts raced through my mind: 'Nine seconds to put gas mask on. Have my soldiers remembered their well-practised drills?' Anyway, having put my gas mask on, I popped my head out into the night. To my eternal relief what I thought had been NBC Chemicals splashing down on our bivouac tent turned out to be rain, and the explosions were those of thunderclaps!

We stayed put until given permission to motor back beside the Main Supply Route past a large prisoner of war cage to the FFMA. Here the Quartermaster of the Queen's Own Highlanders produced a succession of delicious celebratory breakfasts. Somehow he had commandeered, in the best QM tradition, a container lorry full of kidneys and real pork sausages: quite an achievement in a Muslim country!

It was here we heard possibly the most heroic story about any Life Guard member of the ADG. Staff Corporal Evans of our recce troop had broken down, and been left behind with his Scorpion and crew. Somewhere he found a forklift truck, lifted the engine out of his Scorpion, fixed it, and then motored on across enemy territory without marked maps to catch up with the action. Sadly he did not receive official recognition of his devotion to duty.

Eventually we trucked and transportered back to Al Jubayl and Blackadder camp. The RAF flew us home and allowed us probably uniquely to have a free drink: half a litre of German white wine and half a litre of German lager. The only other alcohol we had drunk had been whisky sent to Waterhouse and me through the official mail by Captain (Retired) Simon Hayward!

The other Life Guard who deserves a mention is Major (QM) Chris Slater who was sent with a convoy up the coast from Al Jubayl to Kuwait City to re-establish a British presence. He can therefore justifiably claim to be the first Life Guard into Kuwait City!

Even Headquarters, Household Cavalry, in their offices in Horse Guards felt for a time that they, too, were in action. The Silver Stick

Adjutant, Major Peter Hunter, was on the telephone to Major Ralph Griffin, in charge of the rear party in Athlone Barracks. He suddenly terminated the conversation with 'I must go now, we're being mortared!' The IRA had mounted a mortar attack on the rear of No. 10 Downing Street from a van in Whitehall opposite Horse Guards.

59. Trainer and former Life Guard: Nick Gaselee with 1992 Grand National winner, Party Politics. (*Mike Roberts*)

60. 2Lt Piers German and 2 Troop, A Squadron, Kuwait, 1991.

Chapter 15

Epilogue (1991-1992)

AFTER dealing with the enemy without, on their return to Athlone Barracks the Regiment found that they were faced with the enemy from within: Options for Change.

With the disintegration of the Warsaw Pact and of the former Soviet Union, much of the *raison d'être* of maintaining the 1st British Corps in Germany was gone. The Conservative Government, faced with the chance of reducing the defence spending, accordingly instructed the Defence Secretary, Tom King, to reduce the size of the army.

Although many would have preferred it otherwise, no longer could the two regiments of Household Cavalry rely on immunity from the 1922 amalgamation of The 1st Life Guards and The 2nd Life Guards, nor on the 1969 amalgamation of The Blues with the Royals. The cuts were due, apparently, to come 'across the board'.

Wild rumours started in earnest in the winter of 1990/91 when it was said that Tom King had to be dissuaded from announcing the cuts to the cavalry and to the infantry at the time when a great many of them were on active service in the Gulf.

The facts were that The Life Guards were willing to amalgamate with a regiment of either the line cavalry or the Royal Tank Regiment if this proved possible and if the Regiment's position as Household Troops was safeguarded. The two Colonels implored that, whatever solution was proposed, the position of the Mounted Regiment and its contribution to Public Duties, the Nation and the dignity of the Monarchy should not be affected. This was accepted by the Secretary of State.

Even the columnist Auberon Waugh, a National Service officer with The Blues in the 'fifties, raised the matter in his column in *The Daily Telegraph*.

Then in June, 1991, the proposals were announced: practically every cavalry regiment in the army was to suffer their second amalgamation of the twentieth century. The only sops of comfort that the Regiment could garner were firstly that the Ministry of Defence had decided that both regiments of the Household Cavalry would retain their individual identity, their uniforms, customs and Associations. They must, however, form a Union of one service regiment of two sabre squadrons each and a mixed headquarter element.

Both regiments also drew comfort from the fact that their partners were hardly new, having fought in two World Wars together. The Mounted Regiment, no doubt due in part to their popularity with the British Tourist Board, emerged unscathed, though the viability of keeping them up to strength from a smaller bottom line would be a problem to come.

Ironically the details were announced on the day before Major Ronald Ferguson had organized a charity polo match between officers of the two armoured brigades that had fought in the Gulf. Although leaders such as General Sir Peter de la Billière and Brigadier Patrick Cordingley were present (as were Lieutenant Colonel Mike Vickery, and Major James Hewitt who played in the match), Tom King pleaded pressure of work and declined.

Another question posed was the Household Cavalry's future in Combermere Barracks, Windsor. Home to the various regiments since 1804 when they were built in what today would be called a 'green-field' site, the sixteen acres were now surrounded by prosperous suburbs. Their neighbours were not altogether happy with the various trumpet calls that punctuated the day and with the engine-noises from the CVRs. Freedom of the Royal Borough not-withstanding, the Household Cavalryman in Windsor, though more popular than Kipling's Private Tommy Atkins in times of peace, was a mixed blessing to Windsor.

Back in Germany the Regiment continued to train for their armoured role: their tanks had arrived back from the Gulf by June and required a considerable amount of work on them. In addition there was a large backlog of trade training that was outstanding.

In the summer John Lodge took over from Regimental Corporal Major John Belza; Major Peter Hunter became Second in Command *vice* Major Christopher Anderson; and later Captain Edward Smyth-Osbourne took over as Adjutant from Captain Hugh Robertson.

The Regiment dined out Major General Sir Simon Cooper on his retirement: he had been the second Life Guard to hold the appointment of Major General Commanding the Household Division, the first being Major General Sir Desmond Langley.

For six weeks in the autumn the Regiment were in the field, either firing at Hohne or on exercise for 33 Brigade's annual manoeuvres. Working with the Queen's Own Highlanders in the boggy terrain of the Lüneburg Plain, they had the satisfaction (it apparently was a close-run thing) of seeing elements of the 3rd Royal Tank Regiment, the enemy for this exercise, sink into the morass. The ranges were closed for thirty-six hours while the luckless Royal Engineers, who had done this before, built a road into the bog and recovered the stricken Challengers.

April, 1992, was taken up with preparation for the Regiment's summer visit to Canada for training at Suffield.

In October they came home to Combermere for union with The Blues and Royals to form the Household Cavalry Regiment, a temporary arrangement one must hope.

Regimental Collect

O everlasting God, King of Kings, in whose service we put on the breastplate of faith and love, and for an helmet the hope of salvation, grant we beseech Thee that The Life Guards may be faithful unto death, and receive at last the crown of life from Jesus Christ, our Lord. Amen.

Chapter 16

The Mounted Squadron and the Band

THE traditional role for The Life Guards was, as the name suggests, protection of the person of the Monarch. By the nineteenth century this had become largely symbolic; however, the three regiments of Household Cavalry, rotating between the cavalry (Combermere) barracks in Windsor, and those in Albany Street (Regent's Park) and Hyde Park continued to provide the Queen's (or King's) Life Guard at Horse Guards and ceremonial mounted escorts when required so to do.

The amalgamation of The 1st and The 2nd Life Guards in 1922 led to the surrender of one of the London barracks, initially Hyde Park, but finally Albany Street, the London-based regiment settling into the barracks between the South Carriage Road and Knightsbridge.

The Second World War obviously led to a cessation of mounted ceremonial, with both composite regiments converting to armoured cars and eventually spearheading the rush for Berlin (see chapter one). Knightsbridge (the name by which Hyde Park Barracks is generally known to the Household Cavalry) became a London District store and headquarters mess.

After Victory in Europe (VE Day) there was still the war in the Pacific to resolve. At regimental level nobody had any idea that scientists were working on a new bomb, the use of which on industrial targets in Japan would prompt a speedy surrender. Accordingly Captain Hon. Charlie Mills* and Lieutenants Michael Naylor-Leyland and Dickie Crosfield joined the Commandos. They were training in Wales when, as Naylor-Leyland put it, 'We heard the delightful news that a couple of atom bombs had obliterated a large number of Japs.'

Naylor-Leyland reported to Combermere, and in September, 1945, was sent to Knightsbridge where both regiments, who had by then been told that they were to retain their armoured reconnaissance role for the future, were forming a mounted squadron each. The embryo Household Cavalry Mounted Regiment — the name was changed in the 'eighties to its present title — was commanded by the Silver Stick, at the time Colonel Eric Gooch, whose office was within the barracks.

* Later Lord Hillingdon

His Regimental Adjutant, Major Philip Profumo, managed to combine his duties with those of Master of the Galway Blazers with whom he would hunt twice a week. Majors Neil Foster, a Life Guard, and Tony Murray-Smith of The Blues were the two squadron leaders (both later great Masters of Hounds), and the only other subaltern initially, apart from Naylor-Leyland, was Cornet Lord (David) Burghersh* of The Blues.

Both young officers, one a future Master of the Horse, the other a future Olympic rider, had to go through riding school with the trooper recruits, as has always been the custom since. In the Officers' House matters were not initially harmonious owing to the presence of one Lieutenant Colonel Marcus Lipton of the Royal Army Education Corps and coincidentally Labour Member of Parliament for Lewisham. His left-wing views proving too strong for the Household Cavalry officers, he was rolled up in a carpet and left in it overnight. He seemed to bear a grudge thereafter! However, as the mounted regiment grew, so the London District Officers were moved out of the barracks.

Pitifully few pre-war black horses had been forthcoming from the Royal Army Veterinary Corps Depot at Melton Mowbray, or from anywhere else for that matter. Fortunately Queen Wilhelmina of the Netherlands presented thirty as a gift without which, according to Burghersh's recollection of the event, it was most unlikely that the mounted ceremonial role could have been restarted.

One of the horses, a Hanoverian gelding named Siegfried, proved to be an excellent hunter and ended his days as an unofficial squadron mascot in 1959. In his later days he would be led into the Officers' House dining room on special occasions at the end of dinner (echoes of *The Maltese Cat*), a custom that the old boy appeared to enjoy.

Initially five charming officers and some soldier grooms were seconded from the Polish Carpathian Lancers** to assist Corporal Major 'Tommy' Thompson DCM and the fledgling remount staff in training the new horses.

By the time of the Victory Parade in May, 1946, the Regiment was able to find a Captain's Escort with Standard (three officers, fifty-eight rank and file), though the tunics were still khaki. Full

* Later the Earl of Westmorland

** Poland was a free democracy until 1948 when it became a 'people's democracy' allied to the Soviet Union.

dress started to reappear, in particular for the Musical Ride that went by train to Liverpool.

A full Sovereign's Escort (seven officers and 109 rank and file) was managed for the King's Birthday Parade in the summer of 1947, but come the Royal Wedding in the autumn (Princess Elizabeth to Prince Philip of Greece) the extra demand of a Captain's Escort as well as a Sovereign's Escort led to a cut of a double section in each division in the latter. By command of The King full dress was reissued in time for the wedding (just, we are told), though it was not to be worn by the King's Life Guard until the spring of 1949. (The King's Guards at the royal palaces, provided exclusively by the Foot Guards, had to wait a little longer for the return of their 'Home Service' uniforms and bearskin caps.)

Although the guards at Horse Guards had been composite up to this stage, with the issue of full dress they were henceforth carried out by the alternate squadrons. Although the squadrons were to build up to around 100 black horses each, their current strength today, this was not sufficient for either squadron on its own to supply a Sovereign's Escort. It was therefore decided that the squadrons in turn would 'command' an escort by providing the Escort Commander, the Field Officer, the Standard Party and the two divisions behind the royal carriage: the other squadron would provide the two divisions in front of the carriage and the Serrefile Captain*. A farrier from each squadron, complete with axe and with coverer, rode at the back of the fourth division.

The pre-war cavalry school had been at Weedon. With no horsed cavalry left bar the Household variety, this did not reopen. However, eight-month all-ranks instructors' courses were started at Melton Mowbray to service the Household Cavalry, Foot Guards — various officers were required to ride on ceremonial parades — the Royal Horse Artillery (for the King's Troop, RHA) and the Royal Army Service Corps, who still had a mounted transport company in Aldershot and a mule company in Hong Kong.

In September, 1953, Regimental Headquarters, Household Cavalry, moved out of Hyde Park Barracks to a suite of offices under those of the Major General in Horse Guards, which had been undergoing repairs to bomb damage. The Mounted Regiment came formally into

---

* This officer rode towards the rear of the second division and was responsible, by signalling with his sword, for keeping the front two divisions at the correct distance from the carriage, which set the pace. It only worked if the commanders of those divisions looked over their shoulders constantly, not easy in full dress.

being, the first Commanding Officer as such, rather than the Silver Stick, being Lieutenant Colonel Sir Rupert Hardy Bart, who had rejoined the Regiment during the previous year.

Little has changed over the ensuing forty years, apart from a pernicious growth in administrators. In 1953 the squadron whose parent regiment was abroad administered their band which was based at Knightsbridge: the other squadron administered the headquarter elements, such as cooks, farriers and motor transport drivers, who would be an arbitrary mix of Life Guards and Blues.

There were three attached personnel, apart of course from the Medical Officer and the Veterinary Officer* who were cap-badged as members of one or other of the two regiments: an armourer sergeant from the Royal Electrical and Mechanical Engineers and two corporals from the Royal Army Pay Corps. The days of a Headquarter Squadron, assistant adjutants and lady officers were still a long way away.

Once normality had returned to post-war Britain, the Buying Commission was re-introduced for horses. Run by the RAVC with usually a Household Cavalry representative present, the Commission would travel to Ireland twice a year in search of suitable remounts for the mounted units. Whatever the differences between the British Army and some of the inhabitants in Ulster, the farmer/breeders in the Republic knew on which side their bread was buttered and always ensured that sufficient stock was to hand.

Once in England the remounts would travel first to Melton Mowbray, where they would be turned away for up to a year. Then the blacks (the majority) and the greys (for the trumpeters) would go to Windsor for training by the remount staff before being given the final polish in Knightsbridge. The process for turning an unbroken four-year-old remount into a trained horse capable of carrying a comparatively inexperienced dutyman past cheering crowds and blaring bands took around a year. The band, whose only control of their steeds when playing on the move was through reins loosely tied to their left forearms (in the case of the mounted drummers through reins attached to the stirrups), would be mounted on the older and more sedate animals.

Drum-horses (one per band) are always piebald or skewbald and tend to be massive beasts since, in the case of The Life Guards, the silver side-drums alone weigh a full hundredweight. There was a

---

* Since the 1970s Veterinary Officers have remained as members of the RAVC, but have dressed as Household Cavalry officers.

classic case in the 'sixties when a potential drum-horse, later nicknamed 'Ferguson's Folly' after Captain Ronald Ferguson who had selected it in Ireland, completed full training with the (light) practice drums, only to buckle at the knees when invited to bear the weight of King William IV's silver drums.

In 1954, following the sudden death of Pompey in the previous year, neither squadron had a trained drum-horse to carry the drums on the Birthday Parade. Depending on whose story one hears, either Emperor from One Troop (Corporal Young's recollection), or Zombie from Three Troop (Major Toni Chiesman's version), both black troop horses but 'up to weight', was plucked from the chorus like Thespis and carried the drums with great dignity, though slowly. The Queen, whose profound knowledge of the breeding of horses is well known, became interested in breeding drum-horses in recent years and has provided some to the Household Cavalry and has further potential stock at Hampton Court.

At the end of their useful lives the horses were humanely destroyed, often a source of sadness to many of the soldiers who looked after them. A few, *pace* the 'animal rights' people, went on to charitable institutions such as the Home of Rest for Horses in Buckinghamshire, but after being to an extent institutionalized in barracks, it is questionable if that was the kinder option.

The hooves were often returned, when requested, to the farriers* who would create paper-weights from them. Indeed when the drum-horse Pompey died, from the amount of hooves that went out, for a fee, to the gullible public, the horse must have had as many feet as a centipede.

A hoof was turned up in the tan of the riding-school one morning in the 'sixties by the passing recruits ride, much to the consternation of Riding School Corporal Major 'Jock' Ferrie of The Blues. 'Ride halt! Dismount! Check your horses' feet!' cried Ferrie. It turned out that his dog, Gyp, had secreted the hoof in the tan, having purloined it earlier from the forge.

Training for the men has usually taken around sixteen weeks and starts at Combermere. Regardless of the riding experience of the individual (which is usually zero) soldiers fresh from recruit training, or junior non-commissioned officers from the Regiment, all undergo instruction in stable management, dismounted cavalry drill and equitation. The latter includes jumping both in the covered school

---

* The farriers under the Farrier Major went by unlikely nicknames such as Wally, Sailor and Pablo. As Colonel Darley once put it, they were normally up to some mischief.

and the manège, and across country — not strictly necessary for trotting from Knightsbridge to Whitehall — to give the riders confidence.

The final four weeks of training are carried out in London (the 'kit ride') where the recruit learns how to coordinate himself, the full ceremonial uniform, the highly polished horse furniture and the horse itself into one unit all moving in the same direction and at the same speed.

Manpower is critical within the mounted squadron. The horses have to be looked after and exercised every day either by going on guard or by being taken out at seven o'clock for an hour with the watering order* around the streets of the West End. Any fall in recruiting due to demographic troughs eventually leads to troopers going on guard on the day after they have come off guard, which in turn leads to discontent.

The ceremonial calendar is fairly predictable. Every other day the Queen's Life Guard mounts in barracks and moves to Horse Guards to change with The Blues (later Blues and Royals) in the tilt yard. If the Monarch is in London, it is a 'long' guard (sixteen men), commanded by a captain or subaltern: if not, it is a 'short' guard of twelve men under a Corporal of Horse. The guard spend the night in the guard quarters, the officer having the alternative of either dining with the Queen's Guard at St James's, or entertaining in his own quarters above the guard room. Most opt for the latter.

The only break in this routine is summer camp. Until the 'seventies each squadron would depart in turn by road to Pirbright, a distance of about thirty-five miles which would take some seven hours. (The older horses came down by train.) The horses would be kept tethered on picquet lines — surely now a lost art — and all ranks slept under canvas at Stoney Castle camp. The days were taken up with riding across the training areas and ranges (the latter proved less popular after Corporal of Horse Moss-Norbury was shot in the arm by an inaccurate — or surprisingly accurate — Foot Guard recruit) and in the annual firing with personal weapons.

The nights saw the usual rounds of liquid entertainment between the various messes and usually an all ranks ball in the NAAFI marquee. Summer camp was the high point of the year for men and horses. In the 'seventies the King's Troop, RHA, volunteered to undertake the Queen's Life Guard to enable the Regiment to get

---

* The name for the hourly early morning exercise derives from the time when the horses had to be taken out of barracks in order to be watered.

away en bloc . Summer camps, with all of the horses moved by motor transport, now take place at a variety of locations around the country.

The provision of a Sovereign's Escort, apart from taking the Monarch to and from the Birthday Parade, and the Houses of Parliament for the State Opening, usually occurred twice or three times a year for visiting Heads of State. These usually passed without mishap, though extensive and detailed training with the Mounted Police is carried out by the Escort following an incident in the 'seventies when a man shot at The Queen with a starting pistol on the Birthday Parade.

Perhaps the most eventful escort of the period was that for the arrival of Emperor Hirohito of Japan in 1971. Major John Fuller, as the squadron leader of the mounted Squadron, was due to be the Field Officer of the Escort. However, he was usurped by the Silver Stick, Colonel Ian Baillie, who exercised his right to take part. Fuller therefore took the subordinate position of Escort Commander, riding on the left wheel, rather than the right, of the carriage.

Shortly after leaving Victoria Station there was a clang, and a cry from Squadron Corporal Major Bill Brammer, carrying the standard behind the carriage, of 'Sir! I think I've been hit!' The horrified Fuller looked back, saw that his Corporal Major was still upright and holding his station, so had no alternative but to ride grimly on. His place was with the carriage after all. Then, as the escort was proceeding down the Mall towards Buckingham Palace, a man rushed from the crowd towards the carriage. Fuller, with sixteen years of regimental duty, including Aden, Cyprus and Northern Ireland, to his credit, raised his sword and charged him.

The terrified man chucked his coat at the carriage and turned to flee, running straight into the arms of two policemen which undoubtably saved him from injury, at least, from Fuller. He was later questioned by the police and released without charge. And Brammer? The gold-plated lion on the crown which surmounts the Standard's staff, about the size of a cricket ball and twice as heavy, had worked loose and had fallen onto the Corporal Major's back cuirass. It was handed in later by a member of the public.

There were also other 'hardy annuals', such as the Major General's annual mounted inspection in Hyde Park, the dismounted route-lining in Windsor Castle for the Garter Ceremony in June and staircase parties in the House of Lords for the State Opening, and in Buckingham Palace when required. There were also 'one-off' parades, such as the Investiture of the Prince of Wales (in Wales), Royal marriages, State funerals and the Celebration Parade for The Queen

Mother's ninetieth birthday in 1990. A Musical Ride from both squadrons was formed in most years, and travelled extensively as far afield as Madison Square, New York and Berlin, to name but two locations.

Hunting was regarded as character-forming and developing a good eye for country for officers, so during the season, a slack time for ceremonial, most officers would hunt black horses from Melton Mowbray. This was made possible by the incredible generosity shown to them in the late 'fifties by the likes of Lieutenant Colonel Tony Murray-Smith (the Quorn), Major Bob Hoare (the Cottesmore) and John King* (the Belvoir). Life Guard Officers were also lucky during some of this time in that the squadron leader was Major Toni Chiesman who, with troop horses Tatler and Desmond, could show a clean pair of heels to many a thruster across country in High Leicestershire. He encouraged his officers to hunt whenever their duties allowed. His hunting groom, one Trooper Varley, went on to become Captain Alwyn Varley, the Riding Master at Melton Mowbray.

Lieutenant Colonel Mark Darley of The Blues, who commanded at Knightsbridge during the late 'sixties, did much to popularize the sport with the soldiers by authorizing army transport to enable them to ride with provincial packs. Lieutenant Colonel Andrew Parker Bowles OBE of The Blues and Royals furthered this in the 'eighties by deliberately selecting as remounts horses with a bit of natural impulsion to them: though marginally more difficult on parade; the resulting trained horses were now able to compete on equal terms against private horses in shows and events.

It was Colonel Darley who was given the most unusual reply when offering promotion to a lance corporal. He had thought that it was about time that Lance Corporal Jim Fisher, who had been regimental barber for longer than anyone cared to remember, be made a corporal. Fisher, who like all of his ilk had several lucrative sidelines, asked for time to consider the proposed promotion while he consulted his accountant to see if the extra army pay would place him in a higher tax band. (It did not.)

In 1965 the Regiment moved out of Knightsbridge to temporary stabling in Wellington Barracks for five years to enable their eighty-six year-old home to be rebuilt to a futuristic design by the well-known architect, Sir Basil Spence. The final result was not to everyone's pleasing, especially not to the Warrant Officers and Corporals of Horse:

these gentlemen had to vacate their new mess in short order when

* Later Lord King of Wartnaby, chairman of British Airways

the floor became likely to fall into the gymnasium below. (The fault was only discovered when a new carpet was being laid in anticipation of a visit by The Queen.) At the time of writing (1992) further extensive repairs are apparently necessary.

The art of riding horses and looking after them has not changed much over forty-seven years, nor has Knightsbridge.

The Band of The Life Guards, like that of The Blues and Royals, are commanded directly by the Silver Stick. In common with other bands in the Household Division they are always stationed in London District, in the Household Cavalry's case either in Combermere or Knightsbridge. This does mean that individual musicians are able to 'moonlight' by taking evening employment in civilian orchestras and bands, consequently a very high standard of musical artiste can be recruited. The well-known conductor Sir Colin Davies, for instance, opted to do his late 1940s National Service with the Band.

As has been shown in earlier pages, since 1960 it has been the custom for the Band to pay annual visits to the Regiment when the latter are abroad, which tends to be both a big morale-booster to the Regiment and a good community relations exercise with the local populace. Indeed the Band's concert in 1960 in Bad Oeynhausen, the first foreign engagement for Captain Walter Jackson, the newly appointed Director of Music, and in particular their rendering of *Alte Kameraden*, practically brought the house down.

Corporal 'Jock' Gunn, for many years band secretary, recalls that the Band were in khaki until 1950, and even then some of the musicians had to wear troopers' uniforms, there being a shortage of the marginally different musicians' tunics. This was apparently questioned by King George VI when the Band provided an orchestra to play at a dinner in Windsor Castle during Ascot Week. The King also later ordered through his Gold Stick to the Silver Stick (the correct chain of command) that he wished to see the Band of The Life Guards with white plumes in their helmets (like the dutymen) except for the trumpeters who were to retain red plumes. (Life Guard farriers alone wear black plumes with a navy blue tunic.)

The Band used to take part in the International Horse Show at White City, hacking the horses from and returning to Knightsbridge after the evening performance. On one occasion the Director of Music, Lieutenant Colonel Albert Lemoine, elected to make his own way back later on. The Orderly Officer in barracks received a rather concerned call from the Hammersmith Police in the early hours to say that a singing man in uniform on a horse was adrift in their area: could he please be taken home.

When mounted on parade the Band wear an order of uniform which, less cuirasses, is similar to that worn by the dutymen, with aiguillettes of various sizes to denote rank. If, however, they are to be part of a parade where a member of the Royal Family is due to be present, then the tunics and helmets are discarded for the gold state tunics with the velvet caps.

In the 'sixties it was decided that, for the future, a combined band with the two drum-horses should be present on the Birthday Parade: a single mounted band on its own had tended to be dwarfed by the huge massed bands of the Guards Division beside it, and this move slightly redressed the balance.

Although positions such as Band Corporal Major and Trumpet Major are promoted from within the Band, directors of music are usually bandmasters who come from without, the appointments being made by the Royal School of Military Music at Kneller Hall in conjunction with the Major General and the Silver Stick. It is usual for them then to stay with the Band until retirement.

The Band are all fully trained medical assistants. They took part in the ambulance strike of 1989, coping with great skill at traffic accidents, the odd birth, drug-and drink-related problems and potential suicides.

The Band was also an integral part of the London District collection and casualty evacuation system for the 1991 Gulf War.

Appendix I

COMMANDING OFFICERS, QUARTERMASTERS AND REGIMENTAL CORPORALS MAJOR OF THE LIFE GUARDS 1945 -1992

COMMANDING OFFICERS

Apr 1943	- Apr 1946	R E S Gooch
Apr 1946	- Nov 1947	F E B Wignall
Nov 1947	- Nov 1950	E F B St George
Nov 1950	- Nov 1953	E J S Ward
Nov 1953	- Mar 1956	W H Gerard Leigh
Mar 1956	- Nov 1959	A Meredith-Hardy
Nov 1959	- Apr 1962	E M Turnbull
Apr 1962	- May 1964	J P Fane
May 1964	- Oct 1966	Sir James Scott Bart
Oct 1966	- May 1969	I B Baillie
May 1969	- Sep 1971	H D A Langley
Sep 1971	- Dec 1973	S E M Bradish-Ellames
Dec 1973	- Aug 1976	S C Cooper
Aug 1976	- Oct 1978	A J Hartigan
Oct 1978	- Feb 1981	A B S H Gooch
Feb 1981	- Jul 1983	J B Emson
Jul 1983	- Nov 1985	T J Earl
Nov 1985	- Jun 1988	V A L Goodhew
Jun 1988	- Dec 1990	J W M Ellery
Dec 1990	- Oct 1992	A P De Ritter

QUARTERMASTERS

Apr 1941	- Mar 1947	E S Nicholls
Mar 1947	- Jan 1953	W R Bates
Jan 1953	- Jan 1956	E S Nicholls
Jan 1956	- Sep 1960	D G Roberts
Sep 1960	- Jan 1965	A D Meakin
Jan 1965	- Aug 1971	E Sant
Aug 1971	- Mar 1978	D Charles
Mar 1978	- Apr 1981	J L Morris
Apr 1981	- Jan 1985	B P Payne
Jan 1985	- Mar 1987	L A Lumb
Mar 1987	- Sep 1989	J D Knowles

Sep 1989	- Mar 1990	C R Slater
Mar 1990	- Oct 1992	I W Kelly

REGIMENTAL CORPORALS MAJOR

Jul 1945	- Mar 1953	A H Hylands
Mar 1953	- Feb 1957	J H Jenkins
Feb 1957	- May 1958	E Henderson
May 1958	- Mar 1962	E Sant
Mar 1962	- Jun 1965	E O Lloyd
Jun 1965	- Apr 1966	R G Sheffield
May 1966	- Apr 1969	D Charles
Apr 1969	- Dec 1970	C J Roger
Jan 1971	- Aug 1971	J L Morris
Aug 1971	- Dec 1972	L D Stratford
Dec 1972	- May 1976	M Young
May 1976	- Oct 1978	L A Lumb
Oct 1978	- Oct 1980	A Kelly
Oct 1980	- May 1983	J Leighton
May 1983	- Jun 1985	C R Slater
Jun 1985	- Jun 1987	I W Kelly
Jun 1987	- Jun 1989	A J Mead
Jun 1989	- Jun 1991	J Belza
Jun 1991	- Oct 1992	J Lodge

APPENDIX II

Nominal Roll of A Squadron, The Life Guards, who went into Action in Iraq in February, 1991.

Maj J L Hewitt
Capt R E Mackenzie-Hill
Capt R A E Tarling
Lt T J F C Masterton
2Lt J D A Gaselee
2Lt P G R Earl
2Lt R P G German
2Lt D C G London

WO2 (SCM) Evans D
SCp1 (SQMC) Ormiston D J

CoH Jeram K S
CoH Nicholson C I
CoH Camp S
CoH Godson N
CoH Steed B N
CoH Roberts I
CoH Barry R

LCoH Smithers S F
LCoH Smith R DL
CoH Wells AL
CoH Carter D SL
CoH Douglas WL
CoH O'Connor R D L
CoH Lowe N L
CoH Gandar J
Cpl Stephenson (R A M C)
(with 14/20 RAP)
LCpl Griffin K J
LCpl Vaughan S D M
LCpl Redhead P R
LCpl Roberts P J
LCpl Auld G D

LCpl Bebbington K
LCpl Bright M
LCpl Pellett M J L
LCpl Conway A P
ALCpl Larmouth P
ALCpl Clubley C L

Tpr Abraham A
Tpr Barratt A M
Tpr Bickerdike C R
Tpr Beaumont A M
Tpr Bowden J
(with 14/20 RAP)
Tpr Brown J M
Tpr Carney M
Tpr Carrington P J
Tpr Cochrane J
Tpr Cornock O
Tpr Couling M (Trumpeter)
Tpr Croucher P D
Tpr Davis W M
Tpr Doyle M D P
Tpr Docherty C W C
Tpr Exley R S
Tpr Fitzgerald J
Tpr Fletcher N D
Tpr Gallagher R S
Tpr Garrad M
Tpr Henderson S W
Tpr Tpr Hammond C
Herrero-Driver A
Tpr Hodge K J
Tpr Hopkins L
Tpr Huxley G J
Tpr Horrocks B

Tpr Horvarth D B
Tpr James G H A
Tpr Mahoney W
Tpr Mullins E
Tpr Mather R
Tpr Murgatroyd D J
Tpr Parr J M W
Tpr Penn A
Tpr Pietruszko M R
Tpr Plant S A
Tpr Quartley J M
Tpr Ravenscroft P
Tpr Rees D A
Tpr Simpson D J
Tpr Smith G V
Tpr Squire L D
Tpr Stafford G T
Tpr Stokoe A J
Tpr Taylor A L
Tpr Tomlin K L
Tpr Waller S C
Tpr Williams D
Tpr Wilson A J

REME
SSgt Heywood M
Sgt Needham C
Sgt Greaves P
LSgt Segar P
LSgt Chidgey S
LSgt Chapman J S
LSgt Morrey C I
Cpl Farrell J
LCpl Curry L
LCpl Morris D
LCpl Martin S
LCpl Morris J

Cfn Bamford G T
Cfn Brentley N
Cfn Browne S P
Cfn Carr D
Cfn Chamberlain P S
Cfn Evans R
Cfn Mackie H
Cfn McKeown R

ACC
LCpl Barnard (A2 Echeloncook)

INDEX

(The ranks and titles given here correspond with those held by individuals when last mentioned in the text. Numbers in bold refer to the numbered photographs within the book).